Share Christ

Inviting Others into
Friendship with Jesus

Share Christ

Inviting Others into Friendship with Jesus

Dave Nodar, Dianne Davis,
and Fr. Erik Arnold

**Our
Sunday
Visitor**
www.osv.com
Our Sunday Visitor Publishing Division
Our Sunday Visitor, Inc.
Huntington, Indiana 46750

Nihil Obstat:
Msgr. Michael Heintz, Ph.D.
Censor Librorum

Imprimatur:
✠ Kevin C. Rhoades
Bishop of Fort Wayne-South Bend
February 2, 2018

Except where noted, the Scripture citations used in this work are taken from the *Revised Standard Version of the Bible — Second Catholic Edition* (Ignatius Edition), copyright © 1965, 1966, 2006 National Council of the Churches of Christ in the United States of America. Used by permission. All rights reserved.

English translation of the *Catechism of the Catholic Church* for use in the United States of America copyright © 1994, United States Catholic Conference, Inc. — Libreria Editrice Vaticana. English translation of the *Catechism of the Catholic Church: Modifications from the Editio Typica* copyright © 1997, United States Catholic Conference, Inc. — Libreria Editrice Vaticana.

Quotations from papal and other Vatican-generated documents available on vatican.va are copyright © Libreria Editrice Vaticana.

Every reasonable effort has been made to determine copyright holders of excerpted materials and to secure permissions as needed. If any copyrighted materials have been inadvertently used in this work without proper credit being given in one form or another, please notify Our Sunday Visitor in writing so that future printings of this work may be corrected accordingly.

Our Sunday Visitor Publishing Division, Our Sunday Visitor, Inc., 200 Noll Plaza, Huntington, IN 46750; 1-800-348-2440.

ISBN: 978-1-68192-104-4 (Inventory No. T1839)
eISBN: 978-1-68192-109-9
LCCN: 2018933990

Cover and interior design: Amanda Falk
Cover art: Shutterstock

PRINTED IN THE UNITED STATES OF AMERICA

CONTENTS

Introduction

Dave Nodar

In 1995 I met with Cardinal William Keeler, then Archbishop of Baltimore, to share with him that I wanted to begin a Catholic ministry of evangelization. He was so thrilled to hear that a Catholic was actually evangelizing — and wanting to train others to share their faith in the Lord Jesus — that he immediately recognized ChristLife as an apostolate of the archdiocese.

Since then, ChristLife has experienced the joy of helping many thousands of Catholics personally encounter the Lord Jesus, become his disciples, and joyfully share Christ with others. In addition, ChristLife has trained many parishes and dioceses in an effective process to help the baptized and unbaptized, young and old, hear the good news of God's love and enter into a relationship with Jesus.

This book is the third book in a series: *Discover Christ*, *Follow Christ*, and now *Share Christ*. These books are based on ChristLife's evangelization process used by parishes, small groups, and ministries to begin making missionary disciples.[1] If you haven't read the other two books yet, you may find it helpful to read them before you begin this one, though each of the books stands on its own.

WHAT? YOU WANT ME TO
SHARE CHRIST WITH OTHERS?

For most Catholics, "evangelization" — the word we use for sharing the good news of Jesus Christ with others — is utterly new. The concept may be frightening and foreign to you. The truth is, few of us have received any practical training on actually doing it.

Share Jesus Christ with others? You're kidding, right? How would I start? What would I say? People might think I'm stupid or reject me. I don't have a theology degree. What if someone asks me questions about the Church that I can't answer? No one has ever taught me how to share Christ. Do Catholics really evangelize? This is just a sampling of the thoughts that are probably swirling around your head right now.

Of course, Catholics evangelize. In fact, Catholics were the first evangelizers. Our history of evangelizing goes back to our Lord Jesus, the master evangelizer. His command to the Church is clear: "Go therefore and make disciples of all nations" (Mt 28:19). In fact, the Church teaches that evangelization is "the essential mission of the Church, the reason she exists."[2] At the heart of evangelization is the "clear and unequivocal proclamation of the Lord Jesus."[3]

Bottom line, evangelizing is simply sharing the good news that you have personally experienced. As Pope Benedict XVI said, "The first apostles, like today's, were not heralds of an idea but rather witnesses of a person, Christ. Evangelization is no more than a proclamation of what has been experienced and an invitation to enter into the mystery of communion with Christ."[4]

When I was a twenty-year-old, nominal, agnostic Catholic, I had a radical conversion. I share my full testimony in *Discover Christ*, but basically, once I personally encountered the love of God the Father, the forgiveness of the Lord Jesus, and the power of the Holy Spirit, I was changed from the inside out. My life was turned upside down and right side up. I felt like I was living the scene in *The Wizard of Oz* where the movie goes from black and white to color. Everything changed. I thought, "Why isn't everyone a Christian?" Immediately I began to tell others about the God who loves us and wants us to know him, to know his mercy and forgiveness, and his power to completely change us. I didn't know much, but I was sure there is a God who loves me and wanted everyone to know this good news!

Be available

Let me encourage you with a conversation I had with a faithful, lifelong, church-attending Catholic named Fred. Fred was in his sixties, and the idea of personally sharing Jesus Christ with anyone had never been part of his understanding of the Faith. It never even crossed his mind. However, things dramatically changed for him after he participated in the Christ-Life process at his parish. He not only came into a personal relationship with the Lord Jesus, but learned to share his faith in Jesus with others.

A few months later, shortly before Christmas, Fred's wife "invited" him to go to the mall with her. He later admitted that going to the mall is on his short list of things to avoid, but he reluctantly accepted the "invitation." While at the mall, much to his surprise, he ended up having conversations with two individuals. The first was a Catholic who no longer attended Mass, but seemed to miss being a part of the Church. The second was a single mother whose two sons had both endured major tragedies over the past three months.

In each encounter, he listened attentively, empathized with them, and shared that after Christmas his parish was hosting a seven-week series called Discovering Christ (the first of three courses in the ChristLife series). Each session begins with a free dinner, has teachings on the meaning of life, and presents an opportunity to share in a small group. He told them how the experience of Discovering Christ had changed his life. He then invited each of them to come. To his delight, both were very eager to join him. In both instances, Fred recognized the action of the Holy Spirit in arranging these encounters. They were "divine appointments."

Fred shared, "Imagine my joy at Christmas thinking that I may have brought two people into contact with the Lord Jesus! What a wonderful feeling! And it never would have happened without the training and experience I received in Sharing Christ." Through his experience of sharing Christ with others, he realized he could play a role in helping revitalize his parish. He understood that as a parish they could reach out to others with the joyful news of God's love.

If the idea of sharing Jesus Christ is new to you, it may be helpful to know that it does not depend on your own strength, giftedness, or personality. It is something that Jesus our Lord does in and with us. He uses every personality, with all of our different gifts and quirks, right where we are now. The Lord has strategically positioned you to witness to his good news!

But I'm too busy!

After going through Sharing Christ, another friend, Julie, shared that she had never considered telling others about the Lord Jesus. She went through life thinking that sharing Christ meant adding one more thing to an already busy schedule. However, the course was an epiphany for her because she came to see that evangelizing is meant to be a part of who she is, not something she does occasionally. It has now become something she is aware of all the time, like a radar screen in front of her. She has a whole new way of approaching evangelization. It is now a normal part of her Catholic identity. It's a lifestyle of living for Christ and cooperating with the Holy Spirit — a 24/7 reality. She doesn't feel uptight or pressured in any way, she simply responds to opportunities to share God's love in words and deeds as they present themselves throughout daily life.

That's our hope for you.

Fr. Erik Arnold, Dianne Davis, and I, the authors of this book, are sharing with you from our own experience of sharing Christ with others. We offer you encouragement, examples, and principles more than methods. The Holy Spirit is the one who makes us witnesses of the Lord Jesus, and he will help you to enter into the great adventure of following Jesus as members of his Church and making him known to others.

HOW TO GET THE MOST OUT OF THIS BOOK

We hope this book is more than something you read and put back on your shelf when you're finished. We hope it will inspire you to share the good news of Jesus Christ with others. Here are a few suggestions for getting the most out of this book.

Pray

Prayer is essential to all evangelizing. Ask the Lord Jesus to use your time reading this book to make you his witness. Pray at the beginning of each chapter for the Holy Spirit to inspire your reading and to speak to you through it. Simply tell him you want to be open to all he has for you and all he desires you to do.

Complete the Step into Mission activities

Read each chapter slowly and prayerfully. Take time to do the Step into Mission activities suggested at the end of each chapter. Implement them in your daily life. Make notes or keep a journal as you reflect on each topic and on the suggested actions.

Pay attention to what the Holy Spirit reveals to you. You may recognize his encouragement to change the way you think about something you read. If you notice any resistance or fear about a topic in yourself, stop and pray about that particular area. Ask the Lord for his assistance to see things as he does. If you feel encouragement and resonate with something you have already experienced, ask the Lord to increase grace and awareness in that area.

Thank God for what he is accomplishing in you as you respond to the Holy Spirit's guidance. The Lord wants you to enter into the joy of sharing his love with others. He is faithful. He wants us to share his love with others more than we do, and he will do it through us if we say yes.

Fr. Erik, Dianne, and I, as well as many ChristLife friends from around the world, are praying that your desire to share Christ with others will increase and transform your life as you have the privilege of sharing the love of God revealed in Jesus with others.

There is nothing like seeing the lives of others change from the inside out. It is a result of the divine power of the good news of God's love. It will change you as you have opportunities to share Christ with others. Wait until you see what he has in store for you!

Gather friends

Evangelizing others is hard work without the support and prayer of other brothers and sisters in Christ. Consider gathering together a small group in your home or parish to read through the book together. Discuss each chapter using the questions provided in the Study Guide at the conclusion of this book. Hold one another accountable to the Step into Mission activities.

Share your experience

As the Lord uses you to share himself with others, don't be afraid to share your experience with brothers and sisters in Christ who are also striving to do the work of evangelization. Feel free to tell ChristLife about the opportunities the Holy Spirit provides for you to share Christ with others. Together we can build the kingdom of God on earth!

Your brother in Christ,
Dave Nodar

CONNECT TO CHRISTLIFE

Access additional resources to help you get the most out of this book. Visit: christlife.org/sharechrist.

Chapter 1

Why We Share Christ with Others

Dave Nodar

Let me begin by asking you a question: What does God most want to communicate to all of humanity?

Think about it for a moment and consider what your answer might be.

Some time ago, an American football quarterback, Tim Tebow, became well known as a Christian because of his willingness to share his faith in Christ through the witness of his life and his missionary work with children. He used his platform as an outstanding football player to witness in small ways. For instance, he would kneel in the end zone and pray for a moment after scoring a touchdown. At each game, both college and pro, he would write "John 3:16" in white on his eye black (the black grease players put under their eyes). What happened during one major playoff game was extraordinary. Tim Tebow led the Denver Broncos to a totally unexpected win. More interesting was that many of his statistics ended up using the sequence of numbers 3, 1, and 6. Tebow passed for a career high of 316 yards. His yards per completion were

31.6. His yards per carry were 3.16! The fact that John 3:16 was seen on his face by those watching the game and the coincidence of so many stats using the numbers 316 was not lost on the television or social media commentators. The next morning, millions of people searched for John 3:16, making it the top internet search.

Tebow has encouraged everyone to use whatever position of influence they have to communicate their faith in Christ. He witnesses to Christ by his lifestyle and willingness to share his faith unashamedly in straightforward, simple ways. His use of the eye grease with John 3:16 provoked curiosity among millions of people who then searched for what John 3:16 meant. Who knows what the fruit of that action will be?

THREE ESSENTIAL TRUTHS

Back to the question: What is it that God wants to communicate to all people? The following verse from the Gospel of John summarizes the essence of what God wants every person to know:

> For God so loved the world that he gave his only-begotten Son, that whoever believes in him should not perish but have eternal life. (Jn 3:16)

Let's look at three essential truths communicated in this verse.

For God so loved the world ...

The first truth: God loves you and me and every human being. This is the good news — amazing and potentially life-changing news. God loves *you*! The entire Bible, from beginning to end, essentially cries out, "God loves you!" If this is true, how does

God communicate this love to the world? How can we come to know his love? I mean, really know his love? God reveals his love by giving us Jesus, his only begotten Son.

If you want to know what the love of God the Father is like, look at the Son. Jesus is the perfect reflection of the Father. Jesus tells us, "I and the Father are one" (Jn 10:30). To know what God the Father's love is like, find out what Jesus is like.

Reading the Gospels for the first time as a young man had a tremendous impact on me. Seeing the people Jesus associated with astounded me. Jesus was happy to hang out with anyone who was open to him. He reached out to the poor and to the wealthy: blind Bartimaeus the beggar (Mk 10:46) and Zacchaeus the wealthy tax collector (Lk 19:2). He reached out to people who weren't religious and who were living in serious sin: the Samaritan woman, who had been married several times and was living yet with another man (Jn 4:7–18). He also reached out to the religious: Nicodemus, who was a member of the Jewish Sanhedrin (Jn 3:1). Nobody was excluded from the invitation to come to God the Father through the love Jesus offered to all.

As I read these accounts in the Gospels, I was deeply moved and realized there was hope for me. The Gospels tell us Jesus received sinners (Lk 15:2). Everything that Jesus said and did revealed that no one is outside the reach of God's love. I began to see that God wanted me to come to him through Jesus, whom he had sent.

... that he gave his only-begotten Son, that whoever believes in him should not perish ...

The second truth: Jesus came so that we would not perish. What does it mean to perish? Perishing means being separated from God. The "perishing" this verse is referring to is eternal separation from God — hell. The teaching of Jesus in the Gospels is very clear: both heaven and hell exist.

Who is in danger of perishing? Those who do not believe in Jesus. Because God loves us, he created us with free will. We can choose to live our lives saying, "I will live my way! I'll do whatever I please. I'm not interested in this stuff about Christ, I don't believe it." Or we can choose to say, aided by God's grace, "Lord Jesus, I believe."

As C. S. Lewis famously said, "There are only two kinds of people in the end: those who say to God, 'Your will be done,' and those to whom God says, in the end, 'Your will be done.'"[5]

... but have eternal life.

The third truth: God's ardent desire is for all to be saved. As Saint Paul tells us in Scripture, "[God] desires all to be saved and to come to knowledge of the truth" (1 Tim 2:4). God loves us so much that he sent Jesus on a search and rescue mission to do for us something that we could not do for ourselves. Even more than a parent who longs for the well-being of his or her child, God the Father longs for all to be saved through what Christ has done.

He offers us this free gift of his salvation through Jesus Christ, who died for the forgiveness of our sins and was raised to give us the power to live a new life through faith and Baptism. But it calls for a personal response. Each of us needs to say yes to God through the Lord Jesus Christ.

COMMUNICATING THE GOOD NEWS

How does God plan to communicate this Good News now? The simple answer is: God wants to use each one of us. How do we know? Through Scripture, Church teaching, and the desire of our hearts.

Scripture

Before Jesus ascended to the Father, he said to his disciples: "As the Father has sent me, even so I send you" (Jn 20:21). In the Gospel of Mark, Jesus said, "Go into all the world and proclaim the Gospel to all of the creation" (Mk 16:15). Saint Matthew tells us that Jesus said, "All authority in heaven and on earth had been given to me. Go therefore and make disciples of all nations" (Mt 28:19). Guess what? This mission Jesus entrusted to the Church to go and proclaim the Gospel is a commandment Christ gave to all of his disciples. That means every one of us! Every baptized Christian is called to communicate the inconceivable good news of God's love, revealed in our Lord Jesus Christ, to others. It is at the heart of the Christian faith. Jesus is saying to every one of us who are baptized, "As the Father has sent me, even so I send you" (Jn 20:21).

Church teaching

Since the end of the Second Vatican Council (known as Vatican II) in 1965, all of our popes have been calling all Catholics to embrace the mission of evangelization. It is a radical reemphasis of the mission Jesus entrusted to us 2,000 years ago.

At the conclusion of a Synod of Bishops on evangelization ten years after the close of the second Vatican Council, Pope Paul VI wrote, "'We wish to confirm once more that the task of evangelizing all people constitutes the essential mission of the Church.' ... She exists in order to evangelize."[6]

Saint John Paul II wrote in his 1990 encyclical *Mission of the Redeemer*, "God is opening before the Church the horizons of a humanity more fully prepared for the sowing of the Gospel. I sense the moment has come to commit all of the Church's energies to a new evangelization and to the mission '*ad gentes*.' No believer in Christ, no institution of the

Church, can avoid this supreme duty: to proclaim Christ to all peoples."[7]

LEARN MORE ABOUT THE NEW EVANGELIZATION

Download a free booklet on St. John Paul II's teaching on the new evangelization entitled *Characteristics of the New Evangelization* at christlife.org/sharechrist.

Personal desire

Most of us, once we experience the love of God personally, are anxious to tell others about it. It's like Peter and John in the Acts of the Apostles, "We cannot but speak of what we have seen and heard" (Acts 4:20). It's a natural reaction to share what excites us, much like when we've seen a good movie or a new TV show; we want to tell our friends about it. There is nothing more exciting to share with others than the good news of what Jesus has done for us.

WORD AND WITNESS OF LIFE

The glossary of the *Catechism of the Catholic Church* (CCC) offers the following definition for evangelization: "the proclamation of Christ and his Gospel by word and testimony of life, in fulfillment of Christ's command."[8]

I would like to highlight three key points from this definition:

1. First, we proclaim Christ and his Gospel in word, talking about Jesus and what he has done for us.
2. Second, we share Christ through the witness of our lives, which should be increasingly growing in harmony with God's will.

3. Third, we evangelize because our Lord commands us to do so.

This simple definition clarifies what it means to share Christ. Simply put, both words *and* witness of life are required. Evangelization, furthermore, is a command the Lord gives his Church, not an optional extra for "really holy Catholics."

PERSONAL ENCOUNTER WITH JESUS

When I was a young man searching for the meaning of life, a friend shared with me the change that occurred in his life because of the Lord Jesus. I was impacted by not only his joy in telling me that Jesus had changed his life but also the undeniable transformation of his life. He was different. I had known him for years, but now he had a joy and peace about him that wasn't there previously. He was noticeably free of a lot of behaviors I had been trying to get free of on my own power. He attributed his changed life to Jesus, and he told me that Jesus could change my life as well. He offered a witness both in words and testimony of life.

It is worth mentioning that he evangelized me shortly after his own conversion. It's easy to fall prey to thinking you need to get your life together and receive a theology degree before you can share Christ. Evangelization is not apologetics. It is simply sharing with a friend the love and joy we have found as we continue to grow with Jesus as the center of our lives. If we wait until we become saints, we may never enter into the wonderful mission Jesus has given us.

The Church teaches that the starting point of all evangelization is a person, Jesus Christ, and our relationship with him. This is essential and the very foundation. Evangelization isn't simply sharing what we know about Jesus. It is sharing our lived experience of a personal relationship with Christ.

We cannot give away what we do not possess. The popes in recent years have spoken about this truth many times.

Saint John Paul II said, "The starting point of such a program of evangelization is in fact encounter with the Lord."[9]

Pope Benedict XVI said, "We cannot bring to the world the Good News, which is Christ himself in person, if we ourselves are not deeply united with Christ, if we do not know him profoundly, personally, if we do not live on his Words."[10]

Pope Francis said, "Every Christian is a missionary to the extent that he or she has encountered the love of God in Christ Jesus."[11]

A personal encounter with Jesus is where it all begins. We come to know Jesus personally, and then we are sent forth to live as his disciples and share him with others.

THE FOUNDATION OF EVANGELIZATION

When Saint Paul established the first local churches, he made it clear that Jesus Christ must be the foundation of any church community. "According to the commission of God given to me, like a skilled master builder I laid a foundation, and another man is building upon it. Let each man take care how he builds upon it. For no other foundation can anyone lay than that which is laid, which is Jesus Christ" (1 Cor 3:10–11). Saint Paul wanted the Church in Corinth to be absolutely clear that there is no other basis upon which the Church can grow than the Person of Jesus Christ.

Consider this: You want to build a house with a limited budget, so you discuss cost-saving options with the builder. You're told that building without the foundation is not an option. Without a solid foundation, the house will not last very long against the wind, rain, et cetera. You can't build the first and second floor and forget about the foundation.

While it makes sense to us when it comes to building a physical structure, frequently we want to build up the Church without the foundation. We want to bring people into the first and second floors — teaching on the sacraments, apostolic succession, Mary and the saints, morality — without first laying the essential foundation everyone needs: a personal relationship with Jesus Christ. A huge pastoral problem facing the Church today is the many Catholics who have been catechized but never evangelized. While catechesis is important, it is not the foundation. The Second Vatican Council explains, "In Catholic doctrine there exists an order or a 'hierarchy' of truths, since they vary in relation to the foundation of the Christian faith."[12] The foundation of the Christian faith is a relationship with the Person of Jesus Christ. All evangelization must begin with this core doctrine, which the Church calls the *kerygma*. Pope Francis explains how the Church has recently rediscovered the centrality of this message: "In catechesis too, we have rediscovered the fundamental role of the first announcement or *kerygma*, which needs to be the center of all evangelizing activity and all efforts at Church renewal."[13]

Whenever people encounter the Lord Jesus personally, they want more. They hunger to enter more fully into life in the Church. They desire to mature in their faith and seek to tell others the good news they now know personally. We at ChristLife have witnessed the unbaptized received into the Church. We've seen the baptized who haven't been part of the Church, nor living a Christian life in years, become a vital part of their parish. The foundation of the Church and her mission is the person Jesus Christ and relationship with him. That has to be clear to each of us. This is the basis of effective evangelization.

STEP INTO MISSION

Jesus tells us that "apart from me you can do nothing" (Jn 15:5). The first Step into Mission activity is to pray for your own personal faith renewal and to create a prayer list of people in your life who need to know Jesus Christ. Pause before going to the next chapter, turn to page 89, and complete the Step into Mission activity for chapter 1.

Chapter 2

Befriending Others

Dianne Davis

What images come to your mind when you hear the word evangelization? You may think of Saint John Paul II or Billy Graham speaking to crowds of thousands and thousands of people. Or missionaries giving up everything, life as they knew it, going to some remote area of the world with no water, electricity, or food, to live with pagans and somehow teach them about God.

Or maybe your understanding of evangelization may be more like the following scenario. After a long week, you are looking forward to a lazy Saturday morning where you can sleep in a little later, enjoy some coffee, stay in your comfortable pajamas, and watch Netflix. As you walk down the stairs, you look out the window and see some cars pull into the neighborhood. Out of the cars come teams of people, walking two-by-two to your neighbors' houses. You know who they are. They are the evangelists! As quickly as you can, you close the blinds, turn off any sounds of life in your house, and hide. If they think you are home, they won't leave until you answer the door. You know they aren't Catholic, because most Catholics don't evangelize door-to-door!

Yes, all of these are examples of evangelization. But as Dave mentioned in the previous chapter, evangelization is also meant for people like you and me. Evangelization is not reserved for evangelical preachers, popes, or foreign missionaries.

In his book *Move It Out*, Fr. Tom Forrest wrote the following regarding evangelization:

> Salvation has come, and by some strange and wonderful plan of God, we are its messengers! We have been sent by God himself with the best message ever communicated, and our job is to carry that message not to a particular nation, but to every creature and country of the entire world.[14]

Evangelization is actually the duty and responsibility of all baptized Christians, but don't think of it as a burden. It is an opportunity to be part of God's work! It is sharing God's invitation with the people who are in our lives to have a personal relationship with him. In fact, it's a joy and a privilege!

FRIENDSHIP EVANGELIZATION

The method of evangelization we are presenting in this book is best described as friendship evangelization. Friendship evangelization is usually done one-on-one. It's like sharing with a friend a good book that we've read or a new restaurant we've found. What we are presenting here is simple, and it's something we all can do. We begin with befriending and loving the people the Lord puts in our path.

I was raised in what I considered to be a devout Catholic family. We went to Mass every Sunday. At dinner, my father would often tell us about Jesus' miracles. My sister and I completed religious education and were confirmed. I look back on those years and know I loved Jesus, but I always sensed that there was more and something was missing in my life. I thought I could find the answers in the world through material possessions and my career. I was blessed in many ways with a wonderful husband, two adorable sons, a nice home, and a great career. I had all the things the "world" told me were important. However, inside I knew I was empty, so I began searching for the true meaning of life.

At the time, I was working in banking. One day two women, Deb and Robin, came to my office looking for a commercial mortgage. As soon as they walked in, I knew there was something different about them. Their eyes were bright, and their faces glowed. When they spoke, there was a joy and peace about them that drew me in. I remember thinking to myself, "I'm going to approve their loan, but I'm not letting them leave my office until they share with me what's different about them."

At the end of our meeting I said, "There's something different about you, what is it?" Their response was, "We have a personal relationship with Jesus." This was the first time I had ever heard someone talk about Jesus this way. Intrigued, I invited them to share more about their faith in Christ. They shared the Gospel with me and gave me a simple prayer to invite Jesus into my life. I left our encounter a bit skeptical. I knew my Catholic prayers, but I had never heard of the prayer they gave me. For the rest of the day I thought about what they shared with me, and later that night, after I put my sons to bed, I repented of my sins and committed my life to Jesus. My emptiness was filled with the love of God. My life has never been the same since. I have fallen in love with Jesus. Later I came to realize that the personal commitment I made to Jesus as Lord and the release of the Holy Spirit I experienced in my life were in fact a personal yes to the baptismal promises my godparents had made for me as an infant.

Do you remember the first time you fell in love? Didn't you think about that person all the time? Didn't you want to tell all of your family and friends about him or her? That's what happened to me with Jesus — and it's still happening today, more than fifteen years later!

BEGINNING WITH LOVE

I am not a theologian or Scripture scholar. In college, I took one course in world religions and one in Catholicism, both to satisfy a core requirement for my business and finance major. I share this with you because you don't have to have a degree in theology or any special training to evangelize. All you need is to be in love with Jesus. As your relationship with the Lord grows, your desires will align with the Lord's desires. More than anything, the Lord "desires all men to be saved and to come to the knowledge of the truth" (1 Tim 2:4). The truth is: Jesus loves each of us and wants to be in relationship with us. He spreads this message using us, the people who know him. That's evangelization!

A Scripture passage I believe all evangelization must stem from is, "Love one another as I have loved you" (Jn 15:12). This passage is the foundation, because all evangelization begins with simply loving the people the Lord puts in our path. This includes both casual and intimate relationships. We will meet people in the regular places we visit — the grocery store, our hairdresser, the coffee shop. God has placed many people in our lives: coworkers, neighbors, friends, and, of course, our family. We all know someone in each of these categories who does not have a relationship with the Lord. Some of the people closest to us, those we love the most, will be the hardest to evangelize. Pray for them and ask the Lord for opportunities to talk about Jesus. By the time you finish reading this book, I believe the Lord will open a door for you!

In the Gospels, Jesus shows us many examples of friendship evangelization. In the Gospel of Matthew, to take a key example, God the Father reveals Jesus' identity to John the Baptist, a prophet who has been on the lookout for the Messiah: "And when Jesus was baptized, he went up immediately from the water, and behold, the heavens were opened and he saw the Spirit of God descending like a dove, and alighting on him; and behold, a voice from heaven, saying, 'This is my beloved Son, with whom I am well pleased'" (Mt 3:16–17).

After that, John sent two of his disciples to Jesus. One of them was Andrew, a fisherman, and the other was John. At John the Baptist's insistence, these disciples left him and followed Jesus. After spending the day with him, the first thing Andrew did was find his brother Simon (whom Jesus would rename Peter), and tell him, "We have found the Messiah" (Jn 1:41).

Andrew did not have a theology degree. He was an ordinary person, just like you and me. But once he encountered Jesus and spent time with him, the first thing he wanted to do was share this good news with his brother. Andrew evangelized! Later in the same chapter, John describes the meeting of Philip with Jesus. Once Philip encountered Jesus the Messiah, he told his friend Nathanael. You see the pattern here: it's a friend bringing a friend to Jesus.

Sometimes we have the opportunity to share with and befriend someone who might not look like us, act like us, or be of the same economic class as we are. Consider the story of the Samaritan woman at the well from the Gospel of John (chapter 4). Jews did not associate with Samaritans. Additionally, this woman was an outcast in the town because she was a sinner. She went to the well in the middle of the day, when the sun was hot, to avoid meeting anyone there who would judge her and make her feel ashamed. One day, she met Jesus at the well. Jesus knew all about her. He didn't condone her sin, but he didn't make her feel shame either. He asked her to draw water for him. This is something no one else would do. Immediately, she felt safe and accepted. She began to let down her guard because of the way Jesus treated her. When she realized that Jesus was the Messiah, she left her water jar and ran to town to tell everyone about him. She was open to Jesus because of the way he befriended her by speaking with her when no one else would. This gave her the courage to tell everyone about him, when just moments before she was trying so hard to avoid even seeing her neighbors.

Just like Jesus with the Samaritan woman, in our evangelizing efforts, we need to meet people where they are, with compassion and respect. People will be open to us when we treat them with love and dignity.

AVAILABLE, ANYTIME, ANYWHERE

Scripture reveals many encounters with Jesus, each with different dynamics. That is the way it is going to be for us. Most often, our opportunities to evangelize are going to be with people we meet in our everyday surroundings. There will also be "divine appointments," which come in different forms. The Lord may put somebody in our path whom we've never met before. My suggestion is, as you begin each day with prayer, ask the Lord to fill you with the Holy Spirit so that you will be able to love everyone you meet that day, even strangers. Then be ready to use every opportunity that God gives you to share his love.

I used to be part of a women's prayer group. Part of our prayer included asking the Lord to fill us with the Holy Spirit and arrange opportunities for us to evangelize as we went about our day. Sometimes we would even pray to be so filled with the Holy Spirit that, as people passed us, they would sense that there was something different. After our prayer group, each of us had client meetings, doctor appointments, or various errands — plenty of opportunities for the Lord to work through us.

My friend Cindy often had that prayer answered. One day as she was leaving the market, two men stopped her. They didn't ask her for money. One man simply asked her to pray for the other man! When Cindy told me what happened, she said, "I don't even know how they knew I was a person who prayed. I wasn't wearing anything religious." I know why those men knew they could ask Cindy. It was the Holy Spirit at work, setting up a divine appointment. Like Cindy we are called to live a Triple-A Lifestyle: we need to be available, anytime, and anywhere.

While I was grocery shopping a few years ago, a man named Dennis who was working in the produce department asked if I needed anything. I had seen him often, but this was the first time we had a real conversation. As we spoke, he asked me the same question I had asked Deb and Robin in my office all those years ago: "There is something different about you, what is it?"

Here was my chance to do exactly what those ladies did for me. I shared, "I have a personal relationship with Jesus." He then told me that he had been raised Catholic but hadn't gone to church for forty-five years. After that initial conversation, we talked each time I saw him at the market. We became friends. I even bought a Bible and gave it to him. When Discovering Christ was offered at my parish a few months later, I invited him to come. He came, and before the course even ended he came back to Mass and the Sacrament of Reconciliation. At the Holy Spirit retreat, he committed his life to Jesus. He hasn't missed Mass since, comes to every Bible study we have, and found community in our church. He even has joined our parish's ChristLife team!

HOW WE TREAT PEOPLE MATTERS

If we want to be used by God to evangelize, it's important to spend time with the Lord each day in prayer. Then we need to be prepared and expect opportunities to tell others about Jesus, whether it's a one-time encounter or a slow-growing friendship.

Being available when opportunities come our way is very important. We each have so many things going on in our lives, and we need to ask ourselves, "Am I too busy for others? Am I available when I see someone in need? Do I recognize the prompting of the Holy Spirit and go when he tells me to do something?"

How we treat people really matters. As we treat people with kindness, respect, and love, these casual encounters can evolve into friendships. We need to build relationships of trust before people will feel comfortable enough to share with us the issues that are important to them. Sometimes it happens right away, like with Dennis at the market. Other times, it takes a while. Meanwhile, whether we are aware of it or not, people may be observing us. Are we full of worry and anxiety, or do we handle situations with peace? Do we gossip about other people? Do we share secrets? Do we use words that encourage people or tear people down? Finally, when we find somebody truly in need, do we care enough to actually help them, or are we too busy to do anything?

The point here is that if we cooperate with God and allow him to continue to transform us from the inside out, it will eventually become clear to other people, and they will desire what we have — a personal relationship with the Lord.

When a friend finally begins to open up, it's very important to be nonjudgmental. Once we have earned someone's trust, they may share things they have done in the past or ways they have been a victim of sin themselves. The last thing we want to do is make them feel ashamed. We may even find ourselves in a relationship with someone who looks fine from the outside. It may look like this person has it all together, but they are wounded and broken deep down inside. The reality is that everyone is dealing with something. Many things are visible from the outside — the loss of a spouse or a child, a severe illness, or the loss of a job. However, people's pains will often be internal. Someone may share something with you they have never shared with anyone before because you are the first person to care enough to listen and befriend them.

We all need to learn to be better listeners. This doesn't mean giving advice or fixing things, it simply means listening and genuinely loving the person talking to us. These encounters may be opportunities to share God's love and ultimately invite them into a relationship with him.

ARE YOU READY?

Ask yourself: What keeps you from sharing the Gospel? Is it the fear of rejection or your lack of knowledge of Scripture or theology? Are you afraid you might appear judgmental? When we focus the attention on ourselves, fear can grab hold of us. Satan uses fear to immobilize us. We need to change our mind-set and focus on what Saint Paul says in 2 Timothy 1:7, "For God did not give us a spirit of timidity but a spirit of power and love and self-control." Be confident in God's Word. God will not abandon you. Remember, he is the one who has selected each of us to be part of his mission.

Are you ready? As you were reading this chapter, did the Lord bring to mind some people you know with whom he wants to share his love? It may be a friend or someone you see often but don't know very well. Start praying for them every day! We cannot evangelize without the power of the Holy Spirit. Trust the Lord to go before you and open hearts. Expect the Lord to open doors for you, and then look for those open doors. Don't be so busy that you miss the opportunities. As your friendships with others continue to grow, let people see that you genuinely care about and love them. We are not saved by good works, but our good works flow out of the love we have for the Lord. Put your faith in Christ into action: make a meal, offer a ride to someone, accompany someone to the doctor, be available when they are in need. Or just listen, really listen!

Finally, don't be discouraged when people aren't open to the message of the Gospel. Remember — this is God's initiative. You might be planting a seed that someone else will bring to fruition.

God has given all of us unique gifts. You are an important part of God's plan. Are you available? Are you willing to be one of God's laborers? Jesus said, "The harvest is plentiful, but the laborers are few" (Lk 10:2). Are you willing to be one of God's ambassadors? As Saint Paul says, "We are ambassadors for Christ, God making his appeal through us. We beg you on behalf of Christ, be reconciled to God" (2 Cor 5:20).

STEP INTO MISSION

The second Step into Mission activity is a reflection exercise. Scripture tells us, "But Mary kept all these things, pondering them in her heart" (Lk 2:19). Like Mary, take time to ponder the message of this chapter before going on to the next one. Reflect on how you came to faith in Jesus and how you can grow in your willingness to share Christ with others. Turn to page 90 to complete the exercise.

Chapter 3

Share Your Story

Fr. Erik Arnold

In this chapter, we're going to answer the question, "When I share the Good News in my friendships and relationships, what words do I use?" Let's begin with a powerful quote from Pope Paul VI: "Modern man listens more willingly to witnesses than to teachers, and if he does listen to teachers, it is because they are witnesses."[15] *Encounter*

The difference between teaching and witnessing is profound. When we speak from the heart, from our personal experience, there is an authenticity and sincerity that attracts others and is very powerful in spreading the Gospel. The most effective way to share the good news with others is to use the words of your own story — your own experience of God's love and what the Lord has done in your own life. As Pope Paul VI expressed it, "In the long run, is there any other way of handing on the Gospel than by transmitting to another person one's personal experience of faith?"[16] A teacher can communicate facts out of a book that he or she has not personally experienced, but a witness speaks from the heart, from what he or she has personally experienced.

You might be thinking, "This sounds great, but I don't have a story to share. My life is too ordinary." This simply isn't true. Every one of us has a story, including you. Why? Because God has been at work in your life from the moment he created you, working that you might know him, love him, and experience his gift of salvation. Your life story is built out of all the things the Lord has been doing in your life, both great and small, to bring about your salvation.

KNOWING YOUR STORY

This daily work of God's grace in our lives is never boring. Yes, some people may have a personal story with a little more drama than others. However, each of our stories, regardless of the amount of drama, bears powerful witness to Christ. Take, for example, Saint Thérèse of Lisieux. Compared to someone like Saint Augustine, her life may look incredibly simple and ordinary. She entered the Carmelite convent at age fifteen and after having spent nine years in the cloister, she died at the age of twenty-four. In her short span of life, a priest confessor once reassured her, "Never have you committed a mortal sin."[17] No one would have ever said that of Augustine, whose spiritual life was filled with great drama. But the impact of God's work in Thérèse's quiet and hidden life was so powerful that within years of her death her simple autobiography, *The Story of a Soul,* had become known and loved worldwide.

The point here is that we all have a life story which can reveal the great work and love of God. Each of our stories is different, some have more drama than others, yet the Lord is revealed and made known in each of them in powerful ways.

How do we come to know our story? There are four basic questions we can ask to draw it out:

1. What was my life like before I met Jesus?

By "meeting Jesus" I mean the moment when we chose to respond to his offer to know and experience his love in a personal way and so enter into a living relationship with him. In the words of Saint John Paul II, this is the experience "by which a person is one day overwhelmed and brought to the decision to entrust himself to Jesus Christ by faith."[18] This question is asking, "What was my life like before that happened? What was my life like before my faith moved from my head to my heart, before I had a significant personal encounter with Christ?"

2. How did I realize that I needed Jesus?

Before I met Jesus, what was going on in my life that opened me up to the possibility of a deeper and more personal relationship with him? For some people, it can be the experience of hitting rock bottom and realizing how helpless they are. For others, it can be a slow, steady longing of the heart for something more than the passing pleasures of life. For still others, it can be a moment of tragedy or suffering that jolts us awake. What brought you to the realization that there was something more in life, something that could only be found in Jesus?

3. How did I commit my life to Jesus?

When I realized that I needed Jesus in my life in a deeper way and that I wanted to respond to his love, what did it look like when I committed my life to him? For some people, this happens quickly in a conversion experience similar to Saint Paul on the road to Damascus. For others, it can be a gradual but growing transformation of life and commitment to Jesus as Lord of one's life. How would you describe to others what this looked like in your own life?

4. What difference has Jesus made in my life?

This question is perhaps the easiest to answer of all four. When I look at my life before and after my encounter with Christ, what is different? Am I more peaceful, more joyful, and less anxious now? Do I have a greater sense of purpose? Are old struggles with sin now gone? What differences would others say they see in me and my life?

It is helpful to spend time prayerfully reflecting on these four questions, sketching out the basic elements of your own story, and writing it down. It is helpful to commit all of this to writing for two reasons:

1. We take ownership of it. We are affirming, in faith, "Lord, this is what you've done in my life."

2. We are able to hold on to the details of what God has done for us, so that we do not forget it over time, but rather, appreciate it more deeply in our hearts. Pope Francis tells us, "The joy of evangelizing always arises from grateful remembrance: it is a grace which we constantly need to implore. The apostles never forgot the moment when Jesus touched their hearts: 'It was about four o'clock in the afternoon' (Jn 1:39)."[19]

As you reflect on the four questions above, remember that the story of what God has been doing in your life is bigger than just that one moment in which you first committed your life to the Lord. It is continually unfolding, because God is never finished with you. Your conversion to the Lord is a daily, ongoing work of grace.

A beautiful example of this is Saint Peter, who experienced multiple conversions. His first "yes" to the Lord on the shore of the Sea of Galilee wasn't the only one he would ever offer. There were many other moments when Peter was given the chance to offer a renewed and deepened "yes." At times, he responded heroically, like when many disciples left Jesus but Peter remained, stating, "Lord, to whom shall we go? You have the words of eternal life; and we have believed, and have come to know, that you are the Holy One of God" (Jn 6:68–69). Other times he failed miserably, as when he denied the Lord three times. Little by little, the Lord brought Peter to a place where his "yes" was strong enough to endure even to the point of martyrdom.

Like Peter, our conversion is an ongoing, ever-deepening event in our life. Our story of what God has done for us should reflect this truth. To make sure we don't miss this, there are other questions we can ask ourselves, in addition to the four above, to help flesh out our story and see the bigger picture of what the Lord has done in our lives. For example, we can ask ourselves: What has God taught me from failure? What has God taught me from lack of money? What has he taught me from an experience of sorrow or depression? What has God taught me through waiting? through illness? through disappointments?

An example of my own continuing conversion happened during my first year of seminary in Rome. All of our theology classes at the university were taught in Italian, but I didn't know Italian. I remember my first semester, sitting through theology lectures and not understanding a single word. As the first semester ended and the second began, I remember feeling like I had absolutely no control over my life. During my undergraduate studies, before I entered seminary, I had always done well academically and was able to apply myself to achieve the grades I wanted. Now I seemed to have no control, and everything seemed beyond my ability to manage or grasp. Reflecting on the experience of sitting in lectures that we didn't understand, a fellow classmate of mine summed up the experience best when he said, "I feel like a dog watching television." That expression humorously captures the very painful and dramatic loss of control I felt. As painful as it was, I am certain that I experienced more spiritual growth that year than perhaps any other year up to that point. The growth came because I was forced into a situation in which I could no longer rely on myself, as I was used to doing. I had to learn to rely on the Lord in a new and deeper way. As I look back on that experience of my first year in the seminary in Rome, I can see how my conversion was taken to a deeper place.

SHARING YOUR STORY

After reflecting and praying on what the Lord has been doing in our lives, we come to the next step: sharing our story in our everyday friendships and relationships. We need to trust that the Lord will provide opportunities for that to happen in ways that aren't forced or artificial. We also need to be open and attentive to when those moments arrive. This begins with our own readiness to listen to others and know when they may be opening a door for us to go deeper.

For example, in the workplace we are used to greeting one another with simple, rote exchanges that don't go very deep: "How are you?" "Fine, thanks." Then we move on. There are times, however, when a coworker or neighbor may respond in a way that invites a deeper conversation. We may be expecting them to say, "I'm fine," but instead they respond with "I'm okay ...," and the look on their face tells us there is more going on. In that moment, we need to be attentive and see that we are being invited to go deeper with a follow-up question. As we respond with something as simple as, "Oh, what's going on? You look a little troubled," we may learn much more about what's going on in their life. In all of this, we may be presented with the opportunity to share some of our own story and encourage them by witnessing to God's great love, unfailing care, and boundless mercy.

As we prayerfully look for opportunities to share our story in everyday life, there are some important rules we need to keep in mind:

Rule #1: Make a friend before you make a convert.

Our first aim and goal must always be to love the people God has put into our lives as genuinely and sincerely as we can. In other words, let the relationships and friendships be an end in themselves, rather than treating them as a means to an end (like trying to get as many converts as we can). Conversion may happen as we are given opportunities to share what God has done in our own life and something is sparked in the heart of a friend. However, our first goal must be to sincerely love others before all else. When we make this our first aim, it gives the Lord room to be at work through that love, to accomplish the things that he alone can accomplish.

I was reminded of this rule several years ago when I celebrated the funeral Mass of a young woman in my parish. At the end of the funeral reception, one of the family members gave me a ride back to the parish. I previously learned from a family member that the person driving me had stopped going to Mass many years ago because of a falling-out with the Church. I didn't know the whole story, but I did know that a fifteen-minute ride home to the parish probably wasn't the time to raise the issue, especially in the midst of his grief and sadness. So, I made the decision to simply be as present and loving as I could be. My only agenda during the ride was to befriend him. We talked during the ride home, and when he dropped me off I promised him and his family my prayers.

About six months later, I saw him at a parish event and it dawned on me that I had also seen him recently at Mass. At this particular parish event, he pulled me aside and told me, "Father, I want you to know that you're the reason why I started coming back to Mass." To this day, I don't know exactly what it was during the fifteen-minute drive that helped him make the return to the Lord and the Church. But I do know this: if I had tried on my own to come up with the perfect fifteen-minute conversation to bring him back to the Lord, it would have been a complete failure. Instead, the Lord pushed me to love and befriend him first and so leave room for the Lord to work through that — and he did.

The rule here is simple: let genuine love of others' needs be our first aim, and not simply trying to "win" another convert.

Rule #2: Be yourself.

When you share your story with others, be sincere, be genuine, and be yourself. Our world is hungry for authenticity and sincerity. People will notice and pay attention when you speak from the heart. On the other hand, if they perceive that what you're saying isn't really who you are, or that it's fake in any way, then they won't be interested in hearing what you have to say.

Rule #3: Keep it simple.

In sharing your story with others, remember that there is no need to use high and lofty Christian vocabulary or "church talk" that others probably won't understand. Keep your story simple and use everyday language.

One day during my seminary studies in Rome, I needed to take a taxi across town. I was wearing my clerical "priest clothes," and during the ride the taxi driver asked me in Italian, "So why did you want to become a priest?" I wanted to respond in great detail, but my limited Italian forced me to use the most basic words to share my story with him. I imagine I must have sounded something like Tarzan as I grunted out simple words trying to share my story: "Heart empty — heart want more — Jesus put love in my heart." But as simple as it was, the taxi driver's follow-up questions made me realize that I had been able to communicate in a very basic way what God had done for me. The lesson in that experience was clear: we don't need a high and lofty vocabulary or fancy words to communicate what God has done for us. In fact, it's usually better to keep it simple.

Rule #4: It is God, not we, who changes the heart.
As we share our story, we need to remember the Lord alone changes hearts. We can never force it or make it happen by our own power. Our role is simply to witness to what God has done in our lives and trust that he is working in the hearts of those to whom we are speaking. Rick Warren puts it this way:

> This is the essence of witnessing: simply sharing your personal experiences regarding the Lord. In a courtroom, a witness is not expected to argue the case, prove the truth, or press for a verdict; that is the job of attorneys. Witnesses simply report what has happened.... You may not be a Bible scholar, but you are the authority on your own life, and it's hard to argue with personal experience. In truth, your personal testimony is more effective than a sermon because unbelievers see pastors as professional salesmen, but see you as a satisfied customer so they give you more credibility.[20]

Our role is simple: bear witness to what God has done in our own lives. It is the Lord's role to change the hearts of those who hear us.

Rule #5: *When sharing your story, remember you are fishing, not hunting.*

There's a big difference between hunting and fishing. Hunting often involves stalking, pursuing, tracking, and pulling the trigger in order to capture the prey. Fishing, on the other hand, is less about the pursuit and more about attracting and enticing. In the work of evangelization, we need to see ourselves as "fishers of men" and not "hunters of men."

I once heard a priest share his personal doubts that the Lord could use him in the work of evangelization. He was thinking of evangelization more in terms of hunting and often asked the question, "Lord, do I have all of the gifts, talents, and qualities that I need to do that?" He finally arrived at a place of peace when he understood evangelization to be more like fishing than hunting. He accepted, in faith, that being the man and the priest that God had made him to be was enough to attract people to the Lord.

"Like it or not," he mused, "I am the worm on God's hook and he has cast me into the world to attract people to him." He came to believe that the Lord gave him the gifts and talents needed to attract people to the Faith. In this, he discovered a much greater freedom and joy in being "the worm on God's hook" than in trying to be a hunter. As you share your story with others, trust that the Lord will use your life and your story to attract them to himself, without your having to stalk, pursue, or set traps to win others over.

Rule #6: Respond to others when they open the door to you.

Be attentive to those moments when the door may open for you to take a conversation deeper and so share some of your story to encourage or inspire others. Earlier we used the example of the workplace and what a simple opening in the conversation might look like. This rule calls us to be attentive and open to the Holy Spirit in our day-to-day interactions with others, so that we might recognize when someone is opening the door to go deeper. When we are attentive to the Holy Spirit in this way, it often happens that the Lord provides us with numerous "divine appointments."

Rule #7: Practice makes perfect.

When it comes to sharing your story with others, don't stand on the sidelines and wait for the perfect moment, the perfect opportunity, the perfect words, and so on. Remember that practice makes perfect. Simply wade out and let the Lord teach you as you go. The apostles are great models of this. They didn't have it down perfectly themselves, but they were obedient to the Lord as he sent them out, and they returned amazed that the Lord worked through them as he promised. So don't wait for the perfect situation or the perfect words. In faith, leave room for the Lord to work through you, even with your imperfections, worries, and inexperience. Practice makes perfect!

Be encouraged by this truth: there is great power in your story when you share it with others. The Lord will use it to draw others into his Kingdom, so that they might come to know and experience the same love that you have experienced from him.

STEP INTO MISSION

Take the time now to write out your personal faith story. Turn to page 93 to complete the exercise. Keep praying for the people on your prayer and action list!

Chapter 4

The Power to Share Christ

Dave Nodar

I hope that as you have been reading, reflecting, and doing the action items in each chapter you are noticing a change occurring in your heart and mind regarding sharing Christ. Maybe the idea of telling others about the love of God is becoming something you are more open to. Keep praying and asking the Lord to increase your willingness to share Christ.

In this chapter, we are going to look at our need for the Holy Spirit to empower us to share Christ. Before Jesus ascended into heaven, he told his disciples to go back to Jerusalem and wait for the Holy Spirit to come to them. He said, "Before many days you shall be baptized with the Holy Spirit.... But you shall receive power when the Holy Spirit comes upon you; and you shall be my witnesses in Jerusalem and in all Judea and Samaria and to the ends of the earth" (Acts 1:5, 8). These were his hand-picked apostles and disciples, the men and women who spent three years with Jesus. They saw him work miracles, heard his teachings, and were sent out on mission. Jesus molded them. Yet this was not enough. They needed more. They needed the Holy Spirit.

It was after they received "the promise of the Father" (Acts 1:4) that they were able to do what Jesus trained them to do. On the feast of Pentecost, with great signs and wonders occurring, they were all filled with the Holy Spirit and proclaimed the Gospel (Acts 2). They were radically changed from fearful people to conspicuously transformed men and women. Each person was totally changed and emboldened by the love of God to be a joyful witness proclaiming the good news of the Lord Jesus to the ends of the earth. The Spirit of God, the life-changer, had come and changed them from the inside out. The Church was birthed as a missionary people proclaiming good news in the power of the Holy Spirit, seeing thousands receiving the Lord Jesus and being baptized (Acts 2:41).

We are being sent on this same mission today. The Church (that's us) exists to evangelize.[21] We need this same power. Recent popes agree that all evangelizers need the power of the Holy Spirit:

- Pope Paul VI said, "Evangelization will never be possible without the action of the Holy Spirit."[22] That's pretty clear, isn't it?
- Saint John Paul II said, "Jesus entrusts this work [of evangelization] to human beings: to the apostles and the Church.... In and through them the Holy Spirit remains the transcendent and principal agent for the accomplishment of the work .... The Holy Spirit indeed is the principal agent of the whole of the Church's mission."[23] In other words, the work of sharing the good news as Christians happens only through the Holy Spirit, who is in charge of the mission!
- Pope Francis said, "Spirit-filled evangelizers means evangelizers fearlessly open to the work-

ing of the Holy Spirit. At Pentecost, the Spirit made the apostles go forth from themselves and turned them into heralds of God's wondrous deeds."[24]

- The Holy Father encourages us that if we are going to be evangelizers, we need to be open to and unafraid of the third Person of the Trinity, who can turn us into heralds of his saving work.

What does this mean for you and me? How do we tap into the power of the Holy Spirit to evangelize? The Holy Spirit comes to us in the sacraments of initiation: Baptism, Confirmation, and the Eucharist. In Baptism, all of our sins are forgiven. We become children of God as members of the Church and receive the Holy Spirit. Confirmation adds to what began in Baptism. It is the special outpouring of the Holy Spirit, uniting us more fully with the Trinity and increasing the gifts of the Holy Spirit in us.[25]

PERSONALLY RESPONDING TO THE HOLY SPIRIT

Then why are so many baptized and confirmed Catholics not living a fervent Christian life, full of the Holy Spirit? Why aren't more Catholics boldly proclaiming the Gospel like the apostles did after Pentecost? The answer is that many adult Catholics do not have a living friendship with Jesus Christ and have never made a personal ratification of their baptism. Until we make our own wholehearted and free "yes" to our baptism, the grace of this sacrament is unreleased. The Church teaches that two joined actions are required for a sacrament to bear fruit in our lives: God's action (grace), which works through the sacrament, and man's action (faith). Sacraments are not magical rites that act mechanically, without people's knowledge or consent. Their efficacy is the result of a cooperation between the grace of God and free will. To say it more precisely, the fruit of the sacrament depends entirely on divine grace; however divine grace does not act without the "yes" — the consent — of the person.[26]

When adults are baptized, they in faith make a conscious "yes" to the grace of baptism. When infants are baptized, their parents, godparents, and the Church community provide the faith necessary for grace to operate. The expectation is that a baptized infant will be raised in an environment of faith and will grow to make a personal and mature commitment of faith at some time in his or her life. For many today, however, this environment of faith is missing. Many Catholics and other Christians have their children baptized with little or no real commitment to raise their children in the Christian faith. In effect, these children grow up "culturally Catholic," perhaps even practicing the externals of the Catholic Faith, without any real experience of friendship with Jesus Christ.

These children were baptized into the Catholic faith but grow up living on the margins of the Christian life. The New Evangelization, called for by the Church, is primarily directed toward this growing demographic group. These people aren't just poorly catechized, they've never truly been evangelized. They need to be invited to personally ratify the grace of baptism, giving their complete yes to the Lord. For until one makes a free, conscious, wholehearted yes to the Lord, the grace of the sacrament of Baptism is unreleased, like an unopened Christmas gift tucked away in the corner.

This is not a new phenomenon. Hundreds of years ago, Saint Louis Marie de Montfort recognized the very same pastoral problem that we now face regarding the need for a personal renewal of our Baptism:

Is it not true that nearly all Christians prove unfaithful to the promises made to Jesus in baptism? Where does this universal failure come from, if not from man's habitual forgetfulness of the promises and responsibilities of baptism and from the fact that scarcely anyone makes a personal ratification of the contract made with God through his sponsors?[27]

I was raised in a practicing Catholic family. During my teen years, I rebelled and departed from our faith and values. I sought meaning in a lifestyle that held out the promise of life, but over time failed to fulfill the longings of my heart. Through the prayer and witness of family and friends, I recognized the need for change in my life and came to realize that it had something to do with Jesus Christ.

As I shared previously, a friend of mine went through a tremendous change in his life. I noticed that he stopped doing many of the things I wanted to stop in my own life, but didn't have the power within me to do. He summed up this change by saying, "Dave, Jesus changed my life, and he can change yours." Eventually I told my friend I wanted the relationship with Jesus he had, but I didn't know how to get it. He simply said, "Get down on your knees and pray to Jesus." Well, as a Catholic I knew the prayers of the Church — the Our Father, the Hail Mary, and the Glory Be — but he was telling me to pray to Jesus out loud and tell him in my own words what I wanted.

I simply prayed from my heart, "Jesus, help me." I sincerely told the Lord I wanted to turn to him and away from the life I had been living and asked him to help me. I experienced, for the first time ever, the love of God filling my entire being. I knew I was loved personally, forgiven of my sins, and given power to live differently.

It was the beginning of a new life filled with love, great joy, peace, and a clear sense of purpose. I knew that Jesus was the Lord, risen from the dead, and that I was empowered by the Holy Spirit to live a Christian lifestyle.

The fruit of the transformation became evident in the days and weeks afterward. I desired to spend time in prayer. I prayed the traditional prayers of the Church and added my personal conversation with God. The Scriptures came alive to me as though they were written to me personally. I was receiving great grace from the sacraments for life in the Lord. I sought out friendships with others who believed in the Lord Jesus and desired to support one another in living for him. I wanted to tell everyone this good news that God loves us and has made a way for us to return to him through his Son, Jesus. These are the fruits frequently manifested by those who experience renewal in the Holy Spirit.

When I made a decision of my will to turn to the Lord and away from my sins, asking him to be the center of my life and to fill me with his Holy Spirit, it was a renewal of my baptismal promises that released, immersed, and baptized me in his Holy Spirit.

REDISCOVERING THE HOLY SPIRIT

What happened to me has happened for millions of Catholics since Vatican II. It is a clear answer to Pope Saint John XXIII's prayer summoning the whole Church to pray for a renewed outpouring of the Holy Spirit at the convening of the Council: "Renew your wonders in this our time, as by a new Pentecost."[28] It is the same prayer and cry of all the subsequent popes, praying for a new Pentecost in the Church. What we see occurring is a growing recognition of the need for a personal, renewed commitment of our baptismal promises to Jesus, asking him to be our Lord and Savior and truly the center of our lives.

Do you know this reality of the power of the Spirit? It really is essential to living the Christian life and for you to share Christ. Here is Pope Benedict XVI's encouragement to us:

> Today I would like to extend this invitation to everyone: Let us rediscover, dear brothers and sisters, the beauty of being baptized in the Holy Spirit; let us be aware again of our baptism and our confirmation, sources of grace that are always present. Let us ask the Virgin Mary to obtain a renewed Pentecost for the Church again today, a Pentecost that will spread in everyone the joy of living and witnessing to the Gospel.[29]

To summarize: it is the Holy Spirit, alive and active within us, who enables us to know personally the love of God and motivates us to share this love with others. It is the Spirit who sets up "divine appointments" with others who need to know this truth. It is the Spirit who gives us the words to share. Saint Paul tells us that we are ambassadors for Christ, and God makes his appeal *through us* so that the whole world is reconciled to him (2 Cor 5:19–20). God's plea goes out through us.

However, this is only part of the action of the Spirit in evangelization. The Holy Spirit is also active in the people with whom we share this good news. He precedes us to prepare their hearts. He helps them to make the decision to ask Jesus to be the center of their lives. He is the one who gives them the power to become children of God (Jn 1:12). Saint

Paul tells us that one plants and another waters, but God gives the growth (1 Cor 3:5). This is really good news for us. We are not responsible to make anyone commit their life to Jesus. That is the work of the Holy Spirit. We plant and we water. The rest is up to God. This should free us from most of the fears we have about evangelization. All we are called to do is to share our story, to tell others how Jesus changed our life and that he will change their lives as well if they but ask him.

STEP INTO MISSION

Without the Holy Spirit, evangelization is impossible. Pause now and take time to pray for a renewal of the Holy Spirit in your life. Turn to page 98 for guidance for this prayer.

Chapter 5

Presenting the Good News

Dave Nodar

Each opportunity to share our faith in the Lord Jesus with others is a grace given to us by the Holy Spirit to be ambassadors for Christ. As ambassadors, we have the responsibility to deliver the message as given to us. It is the message revealed by the Holy Spirit in Scripture, the same message the Church has been proclaiming through the centuries. This may sound like a daunting task, one that is too much for us ordinary Christians. However, we are not being asked to present all of the tenets of the Catholic faith, but only those basic elements needed to help a person enter into a personal relationship with the Lord.

COMMUNICATING THE GOSPEL

The Gospel is the good news of God's love manifested through the life, death, and resurrection of the Lord Jesus. The Gospel invites all who hear it to repent and believe in the Lord Jesus. This proclamation, called the *kerygma*, is the first announcement of the core truth of the Christian faith about the Person of Jesus Christ and what he has done for us by his life, death, and resurrection. Pope Francis has encouraged the entire Church to rediscover the primacy of this first proclamation:

"On the lips of the catechist the first proclamation must ring out over and over: 'Jesus Christ loves you; he gave his life to save you; and now he is living at your side every day to enlighten, strengthen and free you.'"[30]

This first proclamation or *kerygma* is the core, the kernel, the mustard seed of the Christian faith, which carries with it divine power to transform us from the inside out. Through it we are made new creations and adopted children of God (2 Corinthians 5:17; John 1:12).

Jesus' death and resurrection are essential to our proclamation.

Saint Paul tells the church in Corinth what is most important to their, and our, faith: "For I delivered to you as of first importance what I also received, that Christ died for our sins in accordance with the scriptures, that he was buried, that he was raised on the third day in accordance with the scriptures, and that he appeared to Cephas, then to the twelve" (1 Corinthians 15:3–5).

Christ died for our sins, was buried, and rose on the third day. Our understanding of this is central to the proclamation of the good news. Our acceptance of this message is the basis of our salvation. As Saint Paul writes, "If you confess with your lips that Jesus is Lord and believe in your heart that God raised him from the dead, you will be saved" (Rom 10:9).

This basic profession of faith that Jesus is Lord is the starting point of the Faith. It is not everything the Church believes and teaches, but it is the foundation from which flow the riches of the entire Christian faith. There is much more to living in Christ, but it all starts with the confession that Jesus is Lord, and God raised him from the dead. The vast treasury of teaching and doctrines of the Church flow out of the initial proclamation that Jesus is Lord. With this foundation, people hunger to learn and believe the truths of our faith and are empowered by grace to live them.

Communicating the Gospel in the language of our contemporaries

It is important to learn how to transmit the Gospel in a way that's understandable to our contemporaries. On the tenth anniversary of the close of the Second Vatican Council, Pope Paul VI said that the objectives of the Council are "definitively summed up in this single one: to make the Church of the twentieth century ever better fitted for proclaiming the Gospel to the people of the twentieth century."[31] The whole purpose of the Council was to equip the Church to better communicate the Gospel to modern society. He later addressed the need to relate the Gospel to our contemporaries in language they can understand:

> Evangelization loses much of its force and effectiveness if it does not take into consideration the actual people to whom it is addressed, if it does not use their language, their signs and symbols, if it does not answer the questions they ask, and if it does not have an impact on their concrete life.[32]

Our present culture is filled with many who are not Christian, nor are they affiliated with any religion. They have very little knowledge of or belief in God. A recent survey conducted by the Pew Center on religious affiliation found that 23 percent of the U.S. population now describe themselves as atheists, agnostics, or nothing in particular (also referred to as "nones").[33] They are indifferent to religion. With this growing demographic in mind, we need to better understand the basics of the Gospel ourselves, so we can authentically communicate to our contemporaries.

BASICS OF THE GOOD NEWS

Here is a simple way of understanding the basic truths of the Gospel. This idea occurred to me a number of years ago during morning Mass as the priest was praying the weekday preface for Ordinary Time, number 2 (now the old version):

> Father, all powerful and ever living God, we do well always and everywhere to give you thanks. In love you created man, in justice you condemned him, but in mercy you redeemed him through Jesus Christ, our Lord.

"In mercy redeemed"

The light went on for me as we prayed: this is a great summary of the good news! The four truths presented in this prayer are:

1. In love God created man
2. In justice, he condemned him
3. But in mercy he redeemed him through Jesus Christ
4. Our Lord

I want you to grasp the beautiful and simple way this outlines the good news that every person needs to hear.

A simple way to remember the four truths is to use four "P"s: purpose, problem, provision, and personal response. A more descriptive way to say it is: God's purpose, our problem, God's provision, and our personal response. Let's break it open a little bit more, so you can become more familiar with these basics of the Gospel.

God's purpose: "In love you created man"

Humanity was created in love. God loves the world, his entire creation, especially humanity. We're created unique. He created us in his image and likeness and gave us free will. He wants us to know his love, to love him in return, and to obey him freely. God is calling each of us into a relationship of love with him. That's ultimately what he wants for his creation, but we have a problem.

Our problem: "In justice you condemned him"

Though created in love and for love, humanity chose to separate ourselves from God. We rebelled against him, choosing from the beginning to make ourselves like God — basically saying we can do it better ourselves. The lyrics of an old Frank Sinatra song say it well: "I did it my way." This is what Adam and Eve said to God when they committed the Original Sin. That original rebellion, the choice to go our own way, continues to separate us from God and one another. The result of this sin is visible in all humanity's inclination to sin. A quote attributed to G. K. Chesterton rightly points out, "The doctrine of original sin is the only philosophy empirically validated by centuries of recorded human history."

Our problem is that because of our sin, we are eternally separated from God. Saint Paul tells us "all have sinned and fall short of the glory of God" (Rom 3:23) and "the wages of sin is death" (Rom 6:23). The death that Saint Paul speaks of is separation from God now and in eternity. Once we recognize our situation, our pride comes into play, and we try to save ourselves. We say prayers. We do good works. We strive for nirvana. We develop our own spirituality. We try to get it together on our own terms. But nothing we do on our own power will work. It is impossible for us to save ourselves.

God's provision: "In mercy you redeemed him through Jesus Christ"

What we cannot do ourselves, Christ has done for us. As mentioned above, our own efforts are useless. But God in his mercy sent his Son, Jesus, who gives himself as a ransom for us. He pays the penalty. He takes the hit for what you and I deserve. Scripture tells us: "For Christ also died for sins once for all, the righteous for the unrighteous, that he might bring us to God" (1 Pet 3:18); and, "But God shows his love for us in that while we were yet sinners Christ died for us" (Rom 5:8).

It is God alone who makes it possible for us to be reconciled to himself. Jesus, the Lamb of God, is slain for our sins. The Father has made the way for us to be reconciled and brought back into relationship with him through what Christ has done for us. Saint Josemaría Escrivá writes about God's provision:

> The abyss of malice which sin opens wide has been bridged by his infinite charity. God did not abandon men. His plans foresaw that the sacrifices of the old law would be insufficient to repair our faults and re-establish the unity which had been lost. A man who was God would have to offer himself up.[34]

This is the incredible good news of God's love and mercy in sending Jesus Christ his Son to rescue us. The life, death, and resurrection of Jesus is the basis of our salvation.

Our personal response: "Our Lord"

In the face of this amazing love of God for us, we must make a personal response. It's not enough to know what Jesus Christ did for us. There are lots of people who intellectually know this. They may even know that Jesus is the Son of God, but that intellectual knowledge is not enough. We must respond to the call to believe in him. "But to all who received him, who believed in his name, he gave power to become children of God" (Jn 1:12). The question we must ask ourselves is: Will I personally accept the Gospel?

On the day of Pentecost after the Holy Spirit fell on the apostles, Peter proclaimed the Gospel to the gathering crowd:

> Let all the house of Israel therefore know assuredly that God has made him both Lord and Christ, this Jesus whom you crucified.

> Now when they heard this, they were cut to the heart, and they said to Peter and the rest of the apostles, "Brethren, what shall we do?" And Peter said to them, "Repent and be baptized every one of you in the name of Jesus Christ for the forgiveness of your sins; and you shall receive the gift of the holy Spirit." (Acts 2:36–38)

Those who heard the message and knew it was true were cut to the core of their being by the reality that Jesus was crucified and God raised him from the dead, making him both Lord and Christ. They asked what to do with this revelation. Peter replied that they must repent — turn around, change their thinking about who Jesus is, and be baptized for the forgiveness of sins. Then they would receive the gift of the Holy Spirit. Like the crowds who heard Peter's preaching, we need to make a personal response to the message of the Gospel.

WHY SHOULD GOD LET US INTO HEAVEN?

Archbishop Adam Exner gave a homily about the basis of our salvation at a conference he spoke at in his home Archdiocese of Vancouver, British Columbia. What follows is an excerpt from the homily:

> Suppose that tonight you were to die and you came face to face with God and suppose that God asked you this question: "Why should I let you into heaven?" Think about your answer. I suspect that most of us would respond to God in somewhat the following fashion:

> "I really tried to be good. I tried to be honest. I really tried to be kind. I prayed every day. I went to church regularly. I belonged to many organizations in my parish.... I taught Catechism. I was the Choir Director, or I sang in the choir. I helped clean the church.... I was a good husband or wife or son or daughter.... I was not really that bad you know, but you know, God, I do admit that I wasn't perfect."

> I think most of our answers would sound a little bit like that. What about these answers? It's really quite frightening because they are all the wrong answers, every one of them. Because really what we're doing is, we are asking God to let us into heaven because of what we did, not because of what Jesus did for us....

His salvation is not earned. His healing is not earned. It is a gift, an unearned gratuitous gift. And so, a really right answer that we should give to God (in reply to the question, "Why should I let you into heaven?") should sound something like this: "Because, God, your son Jesus died on the cross for me and rose again, restoring life, liberating all from sin and restoring life; and aided by your grace, by faith, I accept that gift of salvation offered through the Catholic Church. I accept Jesus as my Healer and Savior. That, God, is the reason why you should let me into heaven."[35]

The basis of your salvation is accepting by personal decision the gift that Jesus is offering you through his death and resurrection. That is your entry into heaven. This must be central to our presentation of the Gospel. We should weave this into our story.

Most people believe it is up to them to earn their way into heaven, but this just isn't true. This is why the Gospel is truly *good news*. By learning a basic way to communicate the Gospel, we can help family members, neighbors, and friends come into relationship with Jesus Christ both now and in eternity.

STEP INTO MISSION

An excellent way to learn the four basic truths of the Gospel is to illustrate them in a simple manner. Taking the time to visually communicate the message will help you internalize the message more concretely, so you can share it with others. Turn to page 99 to complete the Bridge Illustration exercise.

Chapter 6

Inviting Others to Meet Jesus

Dianne Davis

Inviting others to meet Jesus and offering them an opportunity to commit their lives to him doesn't have to be complicated.

My father and his siblings were born in Italy. Growing up, we had family dinners with my grandparents, aunts, uncles, and cousins. I was surrounded by great chefs, each with her own recipe for making the perfect tomato sauce. As I began learning how to cook, I would ask my aunts for their recipes. I would take their recipes and experiment by adding my own touch. Often, a good sauce would take a while to prepare. A few years ago, my son came across a pasta sauce recipe from a famous publisher that contained only three ingredients. When he showed it to me, I looked at how simple it was and thought, "That couldn't possibly be good!" But this simple sauce turned out to be delicious! Now it's the only recipe I use.

Just like the sauce recipe, inviting others to meet Jesus Christ consists of just a few basic ingredients.

1. First, you need to have a personal relationship with the Lord. You cannot share what you don't have. What does this mean? It means living as a disciple, fully committed to growing in relationship with Christ and his Church.

2. Be willing to live the Triple-A Lifestyle — being available, anytime, and anywhere. You don't need to be working full-time for the Lord in ministry, but you should be living out your daily life fully surrendered to Jesus. If you are doing this, eventually your transformation will be evident to others.

If you have these basic ingredients, the Lord will use you for the mission of evangelization.

FOLLOW THE PROMPTINGS OF THE HOLY SPIRIT

In Scripture, we see an example of how someone can go about their normal, day-to-day life, be open to the promptings of the Holy Spirit, and go wherever he leads. In Acts 8:26–40, an angel of the Lord appeared to Philip and said, "Rise and go toward the south to the road that goes down from Jerusalem to Gaza." Philip was already proclaiming the Gospel to great crowds in Samaria, but he was obedient, and he went when the Holy Spirit told him to go. On his journey, he met the treasurer of Ethiopia who was seated in his carriage reading from the Book of Isaiah. The Holy Spirit told Philip to walk alongside the carriage, and he did. He asked the Ethiopian, "Do you understand what you are reading?"

The Ethiopian responded, "How can I unless some one guides me?" So Philip got into the carriage and started sharing the Gospel with him. When they came across some water, the Ethiopian said, "See, here is water! What is to prevent my being baptized?" Then Philip baptized him. Because Philip was open and obedient to the Holy Spirit, the Ethiopian man's life was changed for eternity.

You probably won't meet the treasurer of Ethiopia on his carriage ride, but the Lord will bring people into your life. After a business meeting a few years ago, I was walking back to my car and noticed how dirty it was. I decided to go to the car wash. My schedule was packed that day, so I planned to go to the closest place. But as I got into my car, I felt the Lord telling me to go to a car wash about twenty minutes away, so I went. As I was sitting in the customer waiting room, a young man came to me with a special car polisher and asked if he could buff out the white streaks on my right front bumper. I agreed. While he was buffing the car, I started praying for him and asking the Lord to bless him. The longer I prayed, the more I felt the love of the Lord for this young man. When he finished, I thanked him and asked him if he knew how much God loved him. He smiled at me with tears in his eyes. He shared that he had been in a motorcycle accident the prior year, which left him in a coma. The doctors told his family there was nothing more they could do to save his life. However, he ended up having an unexpected turnaround and made a complete recovery. Since his recovery he often wondered if there was "someone up there" who saved him. That's when I had an opportunity to tell him about Jesus and how much he was loved. God used me that day to deliver a message to that young man because I was attentive to his promptings, and I didn't let myself be too busy to do what he asked me to do.

You don't need to worry about who you are going to meet or what you are going to say. The Holy Spirit will always go before you, preparing the heart of the person you are going to encounter. All you need to do is be attentive to the Holy Spirit so that you know when to act. Then, just be natural. Be yourself and be authentic.

Every morning before I get out of bed, I commit my life to the Lord again. I also offer myself for the mission of evangelization. I want to live my life for Jesus and to be used to bring others to him. When you pray like this, expect the Lord to open up divine appointments, because the Lord takes your prayer seriously!

daily

WHERE TO BEGIN

If you are ready to begin inviting others to meet Jesus, start with the prayer list you made in the "Step into Mission" Activity in chapter 1. As you regularly pray for the people on your list, ask the Lord for opportunities to do something with them. It can be an informal get-together like meeting for coffee, having dinner together, or playing golf. It might even be as simple as sitting next to someone at your children's sports games.

Don't begin the conversation talking about spiritual things. Just be yourself, the new person Jesus has been transforming since you committed your life to him. Be a friend and a good listener. The time frame to begin talking about Jesus will be different with each person. You may be able to talk about spiritual things after just a few meetings with one person, and with others it could be months, or maybe never. If our aim is always to love the people the Lord puts in our lives and trust the Holy Spirit, we won't feel anxious. At some point, your friend may ask what's different about you, and you can tell them your story. Don't be discouraged if it doesn't happen. Remember it's always God's initiative. We are just called to be faithful. If we never have the opportunity to evangelize someone we know, we can love these people through regularly bringing them to the Lord in intercessory prayer. We can imitate Saint Monica who prayed incessantly

Be like Saint Monica

for her husband and her son Augustine's conversions — and only witnessed them turn to Jesus and the Church after years of intercessory prayer and her evangelizing efforts.

However, for those relationships that are deepening, you may get the sense that the Holy Spirit is opening their heart for more. For example, you might suggest going to a Christian concert or movie together. A few years ago, I was able to help arrange a private viewing of a Christian movie at our local movie theater. It was a great evangelizing opportunity for a group of us to invite people on our prayer lists.

> **THE POWER OF INTERCESSORY PRAYER**
>
> For further reading on the importance of intercessory prayer, visit christlife.org/share christ.

What are the opportunities in your area? Perhaps your parish is offering a retreat or a Bible study you could invite people to join. You may suggest to someone on your list that they read a book that provides the Gospel message in a simple understandable way (such as *Discover Christ*, the first book in this series), and offer to meet with them to discuss each chapter over a meal or coffee. Keep your eyes open for a Discovering Christ course in your area, which explores the meaning of life in a video teaching and through small group discussion.[36] Invite them to attend or offer to attend with them. If Discovering Christ is not happening near you, consider hosting it in your home, similar to a small group Bible study. No matter what evangelizing activity you are inviting someone to, be sensitive to meet people where they are spiritually. Presume nothing, whether the person goes to church or not.

DON'T LIMIT YOURSELF

Don't limit sharing the good news with the people on your prayer list. We must be concerned that none should perish. That means in your day-to-day activities always be willing to love everyone you meet, and be ready, if the Holy Spirit opens the door, to tell them about Jesus. You may be at a neighborhood party, at work, at a Little League baseball game, or even in line at the grocery store. Smile at strangers. They may start a conversation with you, which will lead to an opportunity to share something about Jesus.

Earlier this year, I was in Madrid helping my son find an apartment. We found an apartment, but the landlord was away on vacation and would not be able to review and approve our application for a few days. If I waited for the approval before buying the furniture, I would be back in the United States before the apartment was set up. We went to the furniture store, and when the sales lady came to help me, I told her our situation, saying, "I'm ordering everything for my son based on faith in the Lord that the application will be approved." She got tears in her eyes, and that opened up the door to talk about Jesus.

Most of what we've discussed in this book falls into the category of "planting seeds." Don't ever put pressure on yourself thinking you need to say or do more to convince someone to turn to Jesus. We can never convert anyone. That's the Holy's Spirit's job. Saint Paul tells us, "Neither he who plants nor he who waters is anything, but only God who gives the growth" (1 Cor 3:7). We can be at peace as long as we do our part.

What happens when someone is ready to respond to the message of the Gospel? On a recent vacation, my husband gave me a spa appointment as a gift. When the aesthetician finished my facial, she said to me, "Mrs. Davis, I sensed something different about you when you entered this room. As I was giving you the facial I felt something special. When I massaged your shoulders and arms, I didn't feel the tension in your muscles like I do with most of my other clients." As soon as she said that, I told her that my life was changed because of Jesus. She listened intently as I shared my story. I sensed that she was open. I told her how much Jesus loves her.

When I asked her if she would like to commit her life to Jesus, she responded, "Yes." I asked her if I could place my hands on her shoulders as she made a prayer of commitment. I told her that the four basic elements of this prayer are:

1) telling the Lord that you are sorry for your sins,
2) asking Jesus to be the Lord of your life,
3) asking to be filled with the Holy Spirit,
4) and finally, saying "thank you."

I told her that she could say this prayer in her own words, or I could lead her and she could repeat each phrase after me. She chose to follow my lead, so I led her in a prayer of commitment that we often use in the ministry of Christ-Life:

Lord God, please forgive me for the things I have done wrong. I turn to you and turn away from sin. (*In the quiet of your heart, pause here and ask forgiveness for anything you know is keeping you from God*). Jesus, please be the center of my life. I welcome you as Lord and Savior of my life. I ask you to fill me with the Holy Spirit empowering me to live as a son/daughter of God. I want to have your grace to truly live a new life. Thank you for hearing my prayer, through Christ our Lord. Amen.

After we finished the prayer, she started crying and said she felt a tremendous sense of peace. I then told her to get connected to her local Catholic church and to find a Bible study.

If an opportunity like this can happen to me, it can happen to you as well. Expect the Lord to use you! If people are open to the Gospel message, rather than leaving them empty-handed, offer to pray with them to place Jesus at the center of their life. While people can certainly pray a prayer like this on their own, praying together with another person is powerful. Jesus tells us in the Gospel, "If two of you agree on earth about anything they ask, it will be done for them by my Father in heaven. For where two or three are gathered in my name, there am I in the midst of them" (Mt 18:19–20).

Finally, after praying with someone, don't leave them on their own to figure out how to follow Christ. Accompany them and personally connect them to a parish community in their area.

PUT YOUR FAITH INTO ACTION

Living as a disciple of Jesus also means putting your faith into action. Look for opportunities to serve others. In Ephesians 2:10, Saint Paul says, "For we are his workmanship, created in Christ Jesus for good works, which God prepared beforehand, that we should walk in them." Service is a way to put your faith into action, and it may open doors for you to share the Gospel.

A few years ago at my church, a young mother with two daughters had a recurrence of breast cancer that spread all over her body. To make this trial even worse, her husband left her. She had to continue working full-time to maintain her medical insurance benefits. Every Tuesday, she had a four-hour chemo treatment. The other four days she would work a full day without a lunch break. She was doing her best, trying to hold her family together and trying to live so her daughters would be okay, but she was exhausted. When some of us at church found out about this, we decided to help her. What does a working mother need, more than anything? Dinner! Twenty women got together to make a calendar where each of us cooked one day a month. We cooked enough so there would be leftovers for the weekend. This continued for eighteen months. We also connected her with an organization that supports women with breast cancer, and they helped to pay the taxes on her house. Later, we drove her to doctor appointments, even when they were out of town. We also took her to healing services. This woman was a regular churchgoer, but she had gone through so many trials in her life, and she thought they were all coming from God. She didn't understand why she wasn't experiencing any victories. She didn't trust God, and she didn't have a relationship with him. But little by little, through the love we all gave her, her heart started to open.

Two days before she died, her sister called and asked me to come over to the house. "She wants to see you," she said. When I got there, I asked, "How can I pray for you?" She said, "I want Jesus to take me to a safe place." Through our love over the eighteen months, love with no strings attached, she felt the love of the Lord pouring through us and out onto her. In the end, she was able to commit her life to Jesus.

I hope that you don't go through an extreme situation like that one, but there will be many other opportunities. Perhaps an elderly neighbor may need her driveway shoveled after a snowstorm, or maybe you know somebody who has lost a job and can't make ends meet. Your love and help can be the start of a relationship. It may lead someone to ask you about the source of your love and kindness. This could be an opportunity for you to share the Gospel with them, and even open them to committing their lives to Jesus.

In terms of generosity, God cannot be out-given. Often we think when we evangelize or serve others that we are the ones giving to the Lord, which is true. But the Lord is so generous and good with his children, he in turn will give you an unspeakable joy when you see others come to Christ. Are you willing to take a chance and try to invite others to meet Jesus?

STEP INTO MISSION

Turn to page 108 for prayer and reflection on how you can live the Triple A Lifestyle: Available, Anytime, and Anywhere. Continue praying for the people you wrote down on your prayer and action list.

Chapter 7

Put Out into the Deep for a Catch

Fr. Erik Arnold

We've led you through all of the basic, practical steps to effectively share Christ with others. Let's end with one final question: As you practice these steps in your daily life, what should you expect? What response should you be looking for and praying for? Should you be cautiously optimistic, or is it better to play it safe and not hope for too much?

Before we answer this question, let's look at the whole work of evangelization through the Lord's eyes. To know how much we should expect from our work of evangelization, it would be helpful to first know how much he expects. We need to make sure we share God's vision for evangelization so that our expectations, hopes, and dreams match perfectly with his.

Consider the call of Saint Peter in Luke 5:1–11. In this passage, we see the Lord's vision for how abundant the work of evangelization should be.

> While the people pressed upon him to hear the word of God, [Jesus] was standing by the lake

of Gennesaret. And he saw two boats by the lake; but the fishermen had gone out of them and were washing their nets. Getting into one of the boats, which was Simon's, he asked him to put out a little from the land. And he sat down and taught the people from the boat. And when he had ceased speaking, he said to Simon, "Put out into the deep and let down your nets for a catch." And Simon answered, "Master, we toiled all night and took nothing! But at your word I will let down the nets." And when they had done this, they enclosed a great shoal of fish; and as their nets were breaking, they beckoned to their partners in the other boat to come and help them. And they came and filled both the boats, so that they began to sink. But when Simon Peter saw it, he fell down at Jesus' knees, saying, "Depart from me, for I am a sinful man, O Lord." For he was astonished, and all that were with him, at the catch of fish which they had taken; and so also were James and John, sons of Zebedee, who were partners with Simon. And Jesus said to Simon, "Do not be afraid; henceforth you will be catching men." And when they had brought their boats to land, they left everything and followed him.

This passage contains both a vision and a call. Peter is called to a new vocation as a fisher of men. To make sure that Peter understands what the Lord has in mind in this new vocation, he is given a vision of what it can and should look like through the miraculous catch of fish. Just as the catch of fish was miraculously abundant, so too will Peter (and the Church) be as he takes up the mission of evangelization as a fisher of men.

It's important that we don't miss this point. The Lord Jesus is not interested in the small, safe catch that one could potentially make in shallow waters. Because he is God, his vision is big. So he directs Peter to put out into deep water for a more abundant catch. In the same way, God wants the nets of the Church to be stretched to the point of breaking with an abundant catch of men and women "from every nation, from all tribes and peoples and tongues" (Rev 7:9).

SHARING THE LORD'S VISION FOR AN ABUNDANT CATCH

The miraculous catch of fish is an image of what can and should happen when we, the Church, lower our nets to share Christ with others. This is incredibly hopeful, because each of us has family and friends who have not yet experienced the Lord's love and mercy in their lives or have strayed from the Faith. Perhaps we've given up hope that they will ever know the Lord or experience his love at work through the Church. This passage calls us back to a place of hope that even those farthest from the Lord are never beyond the reach of his net.

We need this hope. But we also need practical ways to act on that hope. In this passage, we will discover five fundamental truths to help us share the Lord's vision for an abundant catch, one that is able to bring in even those who are farthest from the Lord. As we share the Lord's vision and let him work through us, the catch will be abundant. He wants us not only to say we will try, but to truly know in our hearts that it can happen.

Truth #1: *The Lord calls all of us to evangelize.*

The call to be a fisher of men is given to Peter, who represents every disciple, every follower of Christ (including you and me), called to share in the mission of being fishers of men. I hope, by now, you've become very familiar and comfortable with Pope Paul VI's words: "Evangelizing is in fact the grace and vocation proper to the Church, her deepest identity. She exists in order to evangelize."[37] The Church exists in order to evangelize! We, members of the Church by Baptism, are all called to be fishers of men. So the first and most important truth from this passage is that, like Peter, we are called to the mission of evangelization. Every baptized man and woman is called, regardless of age, state in life, educational degrees, and so forth. Like Peter, we may feel unworthy, nevertheless the Lord calls us and will provide the grace necessary.

Truth #2: *The Lord's vision for evangelization calls us out into the deep.*

The Lord says to Peter, and to us, "Put out into the deep and let down your nets for a catch" (Lk 5:4). The Lord's call requires us to head out into deep water, which means leaving our comfort zones. The water closer to the shore is more comfortable, but there are fewer fish there. The deep water represents the unknown and the unfamiliar. As we move into unknown and unfamiliar territory, we are going to feel uncomfortable. This is true for us personally and for the Church as a whole.

The New Evangelization calls us to leave our comfort zones so the Lord can reach those who haven't fully experienced his love. When we leave our comfort zones — putting the contents of this book into practice within our own families, in the workplace, or in our neighborhoods — we are bound to feel uncomfortable.

Because this is completely new territory for so many of us, it will be unsettling. But this is exactly the kind of situation that forces us to stop relying on ourselves and begin trusting all the more in the Lord Jesus and the power of the Holy Spirit. Being uncomfortable doesn't mean the Lord isn't calling you to it.

In your uncomfortableness, you may be thinking, "I wish our pastor would take the lead, get out there, and start doing this stuff!" Remember that for many of our priests, the New Evangelization is new for them, too. In fact, many of our priests never had a course on the practical aspects of evangelization in the seminary. The "newness" of the New Evangelization makes everyone uncomfortable, clergy and laity alike. Remember that we are all in this together, learning what the New Evangelization is all about. Our discomfort puts us into a place to rely on the Lord in ways we never have before, allowing his grace and power to work in ways we've never experienced.

Know also that there are many parish priests who hope their own parishioners will step out in the workplace, the neighborhood, and within their families, sharing Christ with others so that the pews of the church can be filled. After all, it is the laity who rub shoulders with those who need to be evangelized.

Don't allow discomfort to cause you to shrink back and stay on the dry land of the seashore. Instead, pray that your uncomfortableness will open up new space for the Lord's grace and power to work in you.

Truth #3: If we listen to our feelings, we probably won't head out into the deep.

In Luke 5, we read that Peter and his companions, all experienced fishermen, worked hard all night but caught nothing. They were finished and already washing their nets when the Lord asked them to put out into the deep for a catch. In this moment, we could easily forgive Peter if he said to Jesus, "I'm the fisherman here. I know what I'm doing. I grew up on the water, I've got a lot more experience with this than you do. Trust me when I tell you that there are no fish to be caught today!" Instead, Peter responds with obedience and says, "Master, we toiled all night and took nothing! But at your word I will let down the nets" (Lk 5:5). Similarly, you and I need to allow our obedience to the Lord to overcome any hesitation we have in terms of our feelings and our emotions when it comes to the work of evangelization.

If we only listen to our feelings and our emotions, we won't head out into the deep. Our journey into the deep happens when, like Peter, we respond with obedience.

Truth #4: We need to fall humbly on our knees before the Lord.

Sharing in the great mission of evangelization requires the humility to recognize that we are the first ones in need of salvation. We need to personally seek ongoing conversion, repentance, and transformation. Peter's response to the Lord after the amazing and abundant catch of fish was, "Depart from me, for I am a sinful man, O Lord" (Lk 5:8). Peter knew himself. He knew he was a sinner, and he confessed it. You and I need to fall before Jesus every day and say, "Lord, I am a sinner. I need your grace. Continue to convert my heart."

Why is our ongoing conversion important? First, because our salvation depends on it. And because we need to practice what we preach. Only then will our message reflect the supernatural authenticity that God grants to one who is trying to be faithful. If we are trying to live the Gospel in daily life, the Lord will grant the grace of a supernatural authenticity to our work when we go out and share our story with others. In a world filled with photoshopped images and "fake news," people are hungry for authenticity, sincerity, and reality.

Truth #5: We cannot do the work of evangelization on our own. We are not called to do it on our own.
Luke tells us: "For [Peter] was astonished, and all that were with him, at the catch of fish which they had taken.... And when they had brought their boats to land, they left everything and followed him" (Lk 5:9–11).

They left everything. Not just Simon Peter, but they — the whole group — left their nets and followed him. These men, partners in an earthly endeavor, were transformed when the Lord called them: Simon Peter, his brother Andrew, James, and John. The great truth that we encounter here is that we are not called to head out into the deep on our own. We are called to do it, but not on our own. We need the strength and support of one another.

In this, there is a responsibility shared among those in every state of life — clergy, laity, single, married, widowed, young adults still discerning God's will for their state in life, and so on — the call to evangelization is universal. This is good news, because it means we can rely on and draw strength from one another.

PUTTING THE FIVE TRUTHS INTO PRACTICE

What does it look like when the Church, following the Lord's command, puts out into the deep for a catch? What does the Lord's vision of evangelization look like when it takes on flesh? To answer that question, let's take a look at the story of Saint Juan Diego.

Juan Diego, a peasant from Cuautitlán, an area of Mexico City, was baptized by a Franciscan missionary when he was fifty years old. On December 9, 1531, while on his way to Mass, he heard a burst of birdsong off to the side of the road. As he turned to see what was happening, he saw a woman radiant in light. She identified herself as the Virgin Mary and instructed him to ask the bishop to build a shrine in that place, on the hill of Tepeyac, from which would be poured out great graces.

Juan Diego shared with the bishop what happened. The bishop was a kind man, but he was skeptical. He asked Juan Diego to come back with a sign, some proof to show that the apparition was true and that the request was from the Lord.

On December 12, 1531, Juan Diego encountered the woman again. He told her the bishop's response and she instructed him to go up to the crest of the hill to gather the flowers that he would find in bloom. Despite it being winter, when you wouldn't expect flowers to be in bloom, he was obedient to the Blessed Mother's request. Juan Diego climbed the hill and found roses in bloom, which he gathered and brought back to her. Mary arranged the flowers in his tilma and told him to go back to the bishop and show him the flowers as the sign he requested. When Juan Diego returned, he had to wait for hours before he was permitted to see the bishop. All the while, he kept the roses hidden from everyone.

When Juan Diego was permitted to enter the bishop's study, he opened his tilma and the roses spilled out. Suddenly the bishop, and everyone else present, fell to their knees before Juan Diego as he held his tilma open. To his astonishment, Juan Diego looked down and saw impressed upon the tilma the image of the very woman he had seen on Tepeyac Hill, the Virgin Mother of God.

Yes, the tilma is miraculous. It is still intact almost five hundred years later, yet the material would normally have disintegrated within twenty-five years. Modern examinations cannot determine how the image was created. But an even greater miracle was to come. The bishop responded to the sign and built a church on Tepeyac Hill, where the Basilica of Our Lady of Guadalupe now stands.

Appearances of Our Lady and the shrines built to commemorate them are never an end in themselves. They always point us to Jesus and offer us the opportunity, with Mary, to proclaim the greatness of the Lord. Mary always points beyond herself to the greatness of God and the mission of Jesus Christ. Mary always instructs us, "Do whatever he tells you" (Jn 2:5). Therein lies the far greater miracle. In the course of the ten years after Juan Diego shared his story with the bishop, almost the entire country of Mexico was converted to Christ, some nine million people.

On the day of Pentecost, Peter, filled with the Holy Spirit, preached to the people of Jerusalem. The Acts of the Apostles tells us that three thousand people were converted that day. Amazing! Compare that with what happened in Mexico. In ten years, nine million people came to know and believe in the Lord Jesus. That's nearly three thousand people a day for ten years! Here, in Mexico, was a net so big that the equivalent of Pentecost happened every day for ten years.

How do we know that those conversions were sincere and from the heart? Look at the fruit that was borne in the lives of the people. Aztec religious practice at the time of Juan Diego was built around the regular practice of human sacrifice. As these conversions began to unfold, human sacrifice ceased. The culture in which the Aztecs worshipped was transformed. Human hearts were changed. You know you are dealing with real conversion of heart when culture itself is changed. That is God's vision for evangelization.

The Lord has this same kind of transformation in mind for us. He wants to reach and change the hearts of people so that true transformation of culture can take place.

Looking at Luke 5, we might think, "This is a nice image of evangelization, but the Lord is being a bit dramatic." But when you think about what happened in Mexico with Juan Diego and Our Lady of Guadalupe, you realize that God is absolutely serious about a catch so abundant that the nets begin to tear. That is his vision. This is what God is calling us to be part of.

THE GREAT GIFT OF THE GREAT COMMISSION

The Lord crowns his work of salvation by calling us to share in this work. It isn't enough for him to save us, but he calls us to be coworkers with him in that very work. This is one of the most beautiful gifts God could give us.

Look at what happened in Mexico when one man shared his story. What if Juan Diego hadn't gone to the bishop? What if fear had won out? What if he had thought, "I don't want to look foolish," and remained silent? Thankfully Juan Diego stepped out in faith and obedience. The result of his sharing his story was that Pentecost began to unfold for nine million people. This is our Lord's vision for the New Evangelization. This is the call that you and I have received, the call to share the salvation of Jesus Christ with others.

Now, ask the Lord to pour out on you the blessings and grace you need to share your story with others and take up the mission of evangelization:

Pour out your Holy Spirit upon me now, Lord.
Fill me with the gifts and graces I need, so that
the new evangelization might begin to unfold

in my own family, neighborhood, and parish community. Father, in your love for the conversion of the whole world, pour out your blessings upon me now that I might hear, in a new way, the great call and the great commission of your Son: "Go therefore and make disciples of all nations, baptizing them in the name of the Father and of the Son and of the Holy Spirit, teaching them to observe all that I have commanded you; and behold, I am with you always, to the close of the age" (Mt 28:19–20).

STEP INTO MISSION

This week's Step into Mission exercise is fun. It is called "cardboard testimonies." You'll need to go online to watch the example video, then you get to create and share your own testimony with the world. Turn to page 110 and put out into the deep!

Step into Mission Activities

CHAPTER 1 STEP INTO MISSION ACTIVITY

1. Pray for a personal renewal

All evangelization begins with our own personal encounter with Jesus Christ. If knowing Jesus personally is not a reality for you, it can be. You can renew the graces given at Baptism and Confirmation by asking Jesus to be your Lord and Savior. Simply turn to him and sincerely ask him to be the center of your life. Ask Jesus to release the power of his Holy Spirit given in Baptism and thank God, because he will do it. Pope Francis invites all Christians to make this personal renewal with this prayer:

> Lord, I have let myself be deceived; in a thousand ways, I have shunned your love, yet here I am once more, to renew my covenant with you. I need you. Save me once again, Lord, take me once more into your redeeming embrace.[38]

2. Create a prayer list

Identify the people in your life with whom you regularly cross paths — people who do not know Jesus personally. Remember your family members, neighbors, coworkers, and friends. Place the names of these people in the space below. Commit to praying for these people daily. Ask the Holy Spirit to provide you with opportunities to share Christ with them.

1. *Mark*	6. *Tammy*
2. *Bailey*	7. *Andrea L.*
3. *Eddie*	8. *Katja*
4. *coworkers*	9. *Julia B.*
5. *neighbors*	10. *Rosa*

Nico Brett

CHAPTER 2 STEP INTO MISSION ACTIVITY

Reflect on the following questions in the space provided below:

COURAGE

*Running
Loyola
OLPH*

1. What people and events has God used to help you come to faith in Jesus?
2. In what areas do you need to grow to be a better witness or friend to others?
3. What are the barriers that keep you from befriending others and from sharing Christ?
4. List the group activities that you are part of — book club, little league parents, golfing group, mother's club, et cetera. Consider how you might share Christ with members of these groups, either individually or as a group.

Reminder: Take time to pray for the people on your prayer-and-action list. Consider one step you can take to reach out to one person on your list.

*Father Rufus
Padre Cleidimar
Father Arnold*

Ona
Jennifer
Valerie Spargo
Grace
Stella

Evanglize to Eddie baptize
your children

7-2-18

Tammy - "I miss
you. Stop putting worldly
things as your idol.
Get marriage annulled.
Pray for his soul."

CHAPTER 3 STEP INTO MISSION ACTIVITY

Write your faith story

Our conversion is an ongoing work of God in our life. Like Saint Peter's conversion, ours unfolds over time, and we have many "conversion moments" that are part of the greater overall conversion God is accomplishing in us. Write a three-minute version of *one* of your personal conversion stories. Try to keep it to two hundred to three hundred words max. Really.

- Initial conversion. Saint John Paul II defined conversion as "accepting by personal decision the saving sovereignty of Jesus Christ and becoming his disciple."[39] To guide the development of your testimony, consider these four basic questions:

  o What was my life like before I met Jesus?
  o How did I realize my need for Jesus?
  o How did I commit my life to Jesus?
  o What difference has Jesus made in my life?

- Ongoing conversion. An experience of growth and transformation that can be connected to an event or gradual change and deepening of relationship with God over an extended period of time. Consider this question: What has God taught me through:

  o Failure, disappointment, or illness?
  o Death of a family member, sorrow, or depression?
  o Waiting or lack of money?
  o Other times of trial in my life?

Tips for organizing and sharing your personal story

DO

1. Remember that sharing your story is powerful
2. Be open to the inspiration of the Holy Spirit
3. Share what God did in your life, the good things that have happened
4. Use concrete details
5. Be ready to adapt your witness to the listener
6. Speak confidently, no need for insecurity — you are simply telling your experience
7. Be attentive to the time available (three minutes)
8. Emphasize major points and be prepared to leave out many details
9. Make eye contact with the individual or group
10. Use humor constructively

DON'T

1. Preach or teach
2. Speak negatively about people, institutions, or other churches
3. Lecture — just tell your story
4. Talk all day/night
5. Overemphasize negative or sinful parts of your life
6. Use church jargon, terms, or clichés
7. Embellish the facts

Reminder: Take time to pray for the people on your prayer-and-action list. Consider one step you can make to reach out to one person on your list.

MY FAITH STORY

_____

_____

_____

_____

_____

_____

_____

_____

_____

_____

_____

_____

_____

_____

_____

_____

_____

_____

_____

_____

Pope Benedict quote
about evolution

Please consider sharing your story with ChristLife! We regularly share testimonies from around the United States (and beyond) on our website: christlife.org. Reach out to us using the contact information in the back of this book.

CHAPTER 4 STEP INTO MISSION ACTIVITY

Pray for renewal in the Holy Spirit

Have you been baptized in the Holy Spirit? Would you like to be?

Jesus tells us to ask for the Holy Spirit and assures us that God the Father wants this for every one of us. Prayerfully read the text below:

> And I tell you, Ask, and it will be given you; seek, and you will find; knock, and it will be opened to you. For every one who asks receives, and he who seeks finds, and to him who knocks it will be opened. What father among you, if his son asks for a fish, will instead of a fish give him a serpent; or if he asks for an egg, will give him a scorpion? If you then, who are evil, know how to give good gifts to your children, how much more will the heavenly Father give the Holy Spirit to those who ask him! (Lk 11:9–13)

When you are ready, simply pray this prayer:

> Lord Jesus, I need the power of your Holy Spirit. Release your graces that have been dormant in my life. Bring me into a deeper relationship with you. Empower me to be a witness for you and live a life of love for you and to love others with your love. Grant me graces to grow in prayer, love, and service. I need you, Lord! Come! Baptize me in your Holy Spirit.

If you already know the joy of the Lordship of Jesus and the power of his Holy Spirit, you can pray for a renewal.

You can do this often, even daily. Pray the prayer above or just ask for renewal of the Holy Spirit in your own words.

Reminder: Take time to pray for the people on your prayer-and-action list. Consider one step you can take to reach out to one person on your list.

CHAPTER 5 STEP INTO MISSION ACTIVITY

Practice illustrating the Gospel message

Here is a simple way to present the four Gospel truths we talked about in this chapter. It's called The Bridge Illustration. If you're a visual learner, this may help you understand the four Gospel truths more fully yourself. It may also be helpful to include a drawing in your discussion as you share the good news with others.

Our purpose is to illustrate the four Gospel truths pictorially:

- God's Purpose
- Our Problem
- God's Provision
- Our Personal Response

For each truth, we begin by summarizing the truth and then illustrate it in a simple diagram.

Truth 1: God's Purpose

God created us to live in a relationship of love with him. This was his plan from the very beginning.

> **What to draw?**
> Draw a square and write "Us" on the left and "God" on the right.

Us   **God**

Truth 2: Our Problem

We chose to separate ourselves from God. We rebelled against God and chose to go our own way. This rebellion is known as Original Sin. All of humanity is infected by this original sin. It's the original cause of separation between ourselves and God (our relationship with God was broken).

What to draw?

Draw yourself and the chasm that separates us from God.

As you draw yourself and this chasm, explain that we add to this separation by our personal sin. We may be experiencing personal guilt and shame, broken relationships, a sense of emptiness, or an ache deep within. The point is to make relevant the fact that we have all sinned, and sin separates us from God. Scripture tells us, "Your iniquities have made a separation between you and your God" (Is 59:2). Sin leads to spiritual death, "For the wages of sin is death" (Rom 6:23).

Often, we try to fill this chasm by our own effort with good works, self-improvement books, and acts of piety. The New Testament makes it clear that the basis of our salvation is not good works, but what Christ has done for us. "He saved us, not because of deeds done by us in righteousness, but in virtue of his own mercy" (Titus 3:5). However, in our pride we often think we can tip the balance of the scale by our own efforts.

[handwritten in left margin: 7-2-18 atheists serving in Kolkata]

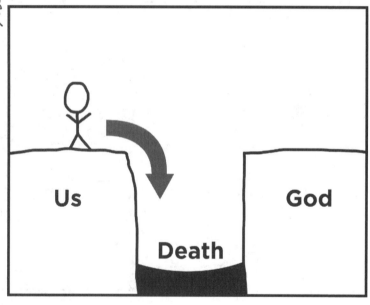

Truth 3: God's Provision

As we try on our own to fix things, we soon find out it doesn't work. God, however, foresaw our disobedience and provided a remedy, his Son Jesus Christ. "But God shows his love for us in that while we were yet sinners Christ died for us" (Rom 5:8). God the Son became one like us, without sin, and he gave himself for our sins on the cross. Only he, who was perfect, could atone for the sins of every human being. It is only through what Christ has done, God's provision, his gift to us, that our friendship with God can be restored.

What to draw?

As you add to the diagram, share that God sent his Son to die on the cross for our sins. Jesus' sacrifice makes it possible for our sins to be forgiven and for us to be reconciled to God. Jesus, and what he has done, is the bridge from heaven to earth. Jesus enables our relationship with God to be restored.

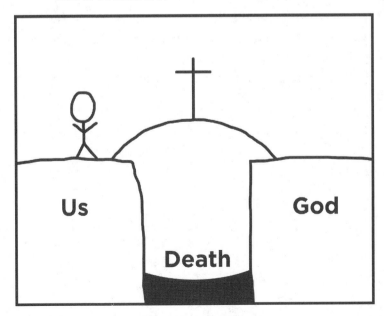

We've gone from the place of God's Purpose (that we live in relationship with him), to Our Problem (the separation our sins have caused), to God's Provision (Jesus enabling our relationship with God to be restored by his death on the cross).

At this point you might ask the person you are sharing with where they see themselves in the diagram. Are they here or there (pointing to one or the other sides of the chasm)? Maybe they are back farther. Perhaps they didn't realize that a personal relationship with the Lord is possible.

Truth 4: Personal Response

It's not enough to know intellectually what God has done for us. This good news calls for a personal response from each of us. We must personally choose to accept the gift that God is offering us through Jesus.

What to draw?

As you complete the diagram, share about the need for a personal response. Knowledge of Jesus' sacrifice is not enough. We need to repent of our sins and personally accept Christ as our Lord and Savior.

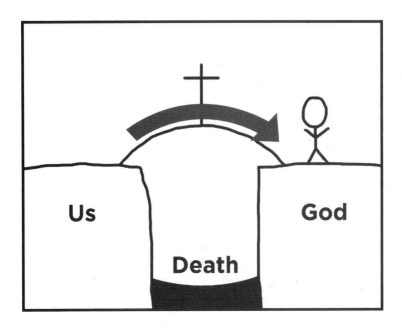

After you've completed the drawing and your sharing, ask the person if they have any questions. Try to answer all their questions. If they seem ready, ask if they would like to cross the bridge and make that personal response to accept God's gift of reconciliation. If they are ready, lead them in a prayer similar to the one below:

> Lord God, please forgive me for the things I have done wrong. I turn to you and turn away from sin. (*In the quiet of your heart, pause here and ask forgiveness for anything you know is keeping you from God.*) Jesus, please be the center of my life. I welcome you as Lord and Savior of my life. I ask you to fill me with the Holy Spirit empowering me to live as a son/daughter of God. I want to have your grace to truly live a new life. Thank

you for hearing my prayer, through Christ our
Lord. Amen.

For those who are already Christians, this act of turn-
ing over their lives to God means returning to Jesus as Lord
of their entire lives. It may mean renewing and deepening
their commitment to him. In addition, for Catholics, it means
taking advantage of the graces available to us in the Church
through the sacraments and having the support of brothers
and sisters in Christ to mature as a Christian.

For those who ask Jesus to be the center of their lives
but have never been baptized, it is crucial to help them connect with the Church to receive the sacraments of initiation
and enter into a community of believers.

Practice the Bridge Illustration

Practice drawing the Bridge Illustration using the box below
while explaining the basic Gospel message. Practicing this exercise will help deepen your understanding of the four basic
Gospel truths and provide you with a tool that you may find
helpful at times when sharing with others.

Reminder: Take time to pray for the people on your prayer-and-action list. Consider one step you can take to reach out to one person on your list.

CHAPTER 6 STEP INTO MISSION ACTIVITY

Start with prayer

Pray for the desire and the ability to live the Triple-A Lifestyle: Available, Anytime, Anywhere. You can use these words, or pray in your own words:

> Dear heavenly Father, thank you for giving me the desire to share my faith. I recognize this is a grace from you. Please fill me with your love. Help me to be available to you at this moment and every moment of my life. I surrender all of my weaknesses and shortcomings to you. Like Mary, I say "yes" to you. Come and fill me with your Holy Spirit and give me a greater desire to evangelize. I ask this in the name of Jesus Christ who is Lord forever and ever. Amen!

Video reflection on being available, anytime, anywhere

Go online to christlife.org/sharechrist and watch the music video "I Refuse" by Christian artist Josh Wilson.

Using the space below reflect on the video using the following journal questions:

- Do you find yourself closing your eyes to the people around you who need Christ?
- How can you be more available to the Holy Spirit's inspiration?

_____

_____

_____

_____

_____

_____

_____

_____

_____

_____

_____

_____

_____

_____

_____

_____

_____

_____

_____

_____

Reminder: Take time to pray for the people on your prayer-and-action list. Consider one step you can take to reach out to one person on your list.

CHAPTER 7 STEP INTO MISSION ACTIVITY

1: Prepare your "cardboard testimony"

We learned what happened when Juan Diego was bold enough to share his story and the impact it had on the evangelization of Mexico. Sometimes, sharing our story in even a simple way can have a profound influence on others. For a moving example of this, look at this video of a group of men and women showing their "cardboard testimonies" at christlife.org/share christ.

A cardboard testimony is a simple and powerful way to share what your life looked like before Jesus and after Jesus (the difference he makes in your life). On one side of the cardboard is a "before" statement that describes your life before Jesus, and on the other side is written an "after" statement, describing how your life has changed because of Jesus.

After watching the video, spend a few minutes thinking about your story and then create your own cardboard testimony. Use it in the step below and share it with the world around you!

TIPS FOR CREATING AND SHARING YOUR CARDBOARD TESTIMONY

- Keep the message short and simple.
- Write legibly and in large letters.
- On Side 1: describe your life before you knew Jesus/without him.
- On Side 2: describe the difference Jesus makes in your life.
- Smile as you turn your cardboard to the "with Jesus" side.

2: Share Your *"cardboard testimony"*

Your story has power, and sharing what Jesus has done for you can have a dramatic impact on others. But where can you share a cardboard testimony with others? Today, with a smartphone or digital camera and the Web, you can put out into the deep and share your cardboard testimony in a big way with the world around you.

Take the cardboard testimony you prepared above and, with the help of a friend or family member and your phone or digital camera, record a short version of your testimony (no more than 3–5 minutes) and share it with others via YouTube or Facebook or another social media platform. As you think and pray about what you'll share, put into practice what you've learned in this book, especially in the Step into Mission activity for chapter 3. Remember, it doesn't need to be professional, just sincere and from the heart. Going public with our faith in this way is a big step, but how will the world know that the love and mercy of Jesus are real unless we share what they look like in our own life? Visit christlife. org/sharechrist to see several examples of individuals who have shared their cardboard testimony online.

> Please consider sharing your story with ChristLife! We regularly share testimonies from around the United States (and beyond) on our website: christlife.org. Reach out to us using the contact information in the back of this book.

Reminder: Take time to pray for the people on your prayer-and-action list. Consider one step you can take to reach out to one person on your list.

Study Guide

The following study questions can be used for small groups or for individual reflection. After reading each chapter, it is best to complete that chapter's Step into Mission activity before your small group discussion.

CHAPTER 1: WHY WE SHARE CHRIST WITH OTHERS

1. What does God most want to communicate with all of humanity? (page 15)
2. Think about your own personality traits, gifts, and circles of influence. How do these help you share Christ? How might they hinder you from sharing Christ? (page 15)
3. Review the three truths outlined in chapter 1. Do you agree with these truths? Have you always? What changed your mind? Which is the most challenging truth to you at this time? (pages 16–18)
4. STEP INTO MISSION (page 89): What are some things that might make it difficult to complete this activity? How do you plan to overcome them?

CHAPTER 2: BEFRIENDING OTHERS

1. A willingness to love others as Christ has loved you is at the heart of friendship evangelization. List the ways in which the Lord has loved you. Reflect on how personal they are. (page 28)
2. Friendship, casual interaction, and social conversation are becoming more difficult in our society today. Think about the excuses you use, or the barriers others use, to avoid eye contact and conversation. Journal or discuss in your group ways you can overcome these in yourself, in others. (pages 28–30)
3. The Triple-A Lifestyle requires a new perspective on your time and resources. As you reflect and pray about this, can you recall any "divine appointments" you have already experienced? How can you be better prepared for the next ones? (pages 30–32)
4. The author reminds us that "Satan uses fear to immobilize us." Recall and journal or share a time when you felt afraid to discuss your faith. How does 2 Timothy 1:7 help you to overcome fear and feel more confident? (page 33)
5. STEP INTO MISSION (page 90): As you completed the activity, what stood out to you about the areas you need to grow in or the barriers you have identified? What concrete action can you take today to overcome this?

CHAPTER 3: SHARE YOUR STORY

1. How do you feel about sharing your personal story with others? Have you ever taken the time to write out your faith story?

2. How do the four guiding questions the author presents help you to share your story? (pages 38–40)

3. "Rule # 1: Make a friend before you make a convert" (page 43) dovetails nicely with the idea of fishing versus hunting (page 46). Have you ever received the friendship of another, and then felt influenced by that friend? Journal or share with your group this experience and how it felt to be sought out and befriended.

4. Review the "Rules" on pages 43–47. Authenticity, simplicity, and love are the hallmarks of an evangelizing story. Reread your story and underline all the words that show authenticity or relate Christ's love. Ask the Holy Spirit to help you add these elements if they are missing.

5. STEP INTO MISSION (pages 93–97): How difficult was it for you to complete this activity? Which parts were difficult? Which prompts from the author were the most helpful? What did you learn about your own conversion journey in this activity?

CHAPTER 4: THE POWER TO SHARE CHRIST

1. Are you aware of any changes in your willingness to share Christ with others? Do others comment on a change in you? Journal or discuss in your group any evangelizing conversations you have had since beginning this journey.

2. Summarizing Pope Francis on pages 50–51, the author concludes, "We need to be open to and unafraid of the third Person of the Trinity." Are you? Make a list of all the things you know about the Holy Spirit, his work, and his gifts. Have you asked Jesus to fill you with the power of the Holy Spirit, renewing your baptismal promises? (page 54)

3. 1 Corinthians 3:5 reminds us that it is the calling of Christians to plant and to water, but the work of the Holy Spirit to give growth. How does this free you from your fears and preconceived ideas about evangelization? (page 56)

4. STEP INTO MISSION (pages 98–99): Review the people on your prayer-and-action list. Journal or discuss any changes in your attitude toward these people. Have you noticed any changes in their openness to your friendship? Do you pray to be available and ready for "divine appointments"?

CHAPTER 5: PRESENTING THE GOOD NEWS

1. Do you agree with the statement on page 57, "We have the responsibility to deliver the message as given to us"? Do you feel you know and understand this Gospel message? Which parts do you struggle with embracing now? Which parts have you struggled with in the past?

2. How can we say God loves mankind if he also condemns us? Reread page 61 and build your response to this objection. Preparing for this question will cement your understanding of God's love for us.

3. God's provision is perfect. "What we cannot do for ourselves, Christ has already done for us." Through the gift of faith we can accept the saving sacrifice of God's Son, Jesus, to redeem our sin. Do you accept this Gospel truth for yourself and believe it also applies to every person and every sin? Do you agree that no sin is greater than the mercy of Jesus Christ if the sinner is truly repentant? (pages 62–63)

4. As you reflect on this chapter, are there people who come to mind who you know would benefit from hearing the Good News?

5. STEP INTO MISSION (page 99–107): Is the Bridge Illustration tool something you think will be useful for personally understanding the Gospel? Do you think it would be helpful at times to share with others?

CHAPTER 6: INVITING OTHERS TO MEET JESUS

1. In your personal relationship with the Lord, are you living as a disciple? Are there areas of your life you have already committed to the Lord? Are there areas or habits you are struggling to commit to the Lord? Journal and pray about these, asking the Lord to assist you in letting go. Share with your group or in your journal how the Lord answers your prayer.

2. What do you think it means to "follow the promptings of the Holy Spirit"? Do you hesitate to submit to the Lord because of fear of what he might prompt you to do? (pages 68–70)

3. Thinking about those on your prayer-and-action list, have you noticed any changes in your relationship since you began praying for them? Have you had any opportunities to share your story with anyone? Have new names come to mind to add to your list? (page 70)

4. For some of the people on your prayer-and-action list, you will never have the opportunity to evangelize them. What should your attitude be for those "never" relationships? (pages 70–71)

5. STEP INTO MISSION (pages 108–109): Think about the Triple-A Lifestyle. Are you feeling an increased desire or openness to serving the Lord anytime, anywhere, and in any way? How did you like the video "I Refuse" by Josh Wilson? Journal or discuss with your group an example of a time when you responded to the Holy Spirit leading you. Journal or discuss with your group how you felt if you later realized that you missed an opportunity to serve the Lord.

CHAPTER 7: PUT OUT INTO THE DEEP FOR A CATCH

1. What is God's vision for evangelization? Where do you see yourself in this vision? What is your response to the Lord's call to be a "fisher of men"? (pages 78–79)

2. Peter was called out to the deep water for a greater catch than he had ever known, and he obediently followed Jesus' call. In what ways have you already felt the Lord stretching you as he calls you out of your comfort zone? Have you seen any fruit come from your obedience? (pages 79–82)

3. What does it mean to be humble before the Lord? Why is humility a necessary step for salvation? How does your prayer life help you remain humble? (page 82)

4. Do miracles happen in our time? What is your attitude toward miraculous stories of conversion or healing? What should our attitude be? Are miracles helpful or not for evangelizing believers? nonbelievers?

5. STEP INTO MISSION (pages 110–111): What impressed you most about the cardboard testimony video? How did it feel to make your cardboard testimony? Do you plan to record and share your own testimony video? If not, why not?

Endnotes

1 Learn more about the ChristLife process at www.christlife.org.

2 Pope Paul VI, *Evangelii Nuntiandi (On Evangelization in the Modern World)*, December 8, 1975, http://w2.vatican.va/content/paulvi/en/apost_exhortations/documents/hf_p-vi_exh_19751208_evangelii-nuntiandi.html, par. 14.

3 Ibid., 22.

4 Pope Benedict XVI, General Audience, March 22, 2006.

5 C. S. Lewis, *The Great Divorce*, Revised ed. (New York: HarperOne, 2015), 75.

6 Pope Paul VI, *Evangelii Nuntiandi*, par. 14.

7 Pope John Paul II, *Redemptoris Missio (Mission of the Redeemer)*, December 7, 1990, http://w2.vatican.va/content/john-paul-ii/en/encyclicals/documents/hf_jp-ii_enc_07121990_redemptoris-missio.html, par. 3.

8 CCC 905.

9 Pope John Paul II, *Ecclesia in America (The Church in America)*, 1999, http://w2.vatican.va/content/john-paul-ii/en/apost_exhortations/documents/hf_jp-ii_exh_22011999_ecclesia-in-america.html, par. 3.

10 Pope Benedict XVI, Address at the Close of the Papal Spiritual Exercises, March 11, 2006, https://w2.vatican.va/content/benedict-xvi/en/speeches/2006/march/documents/hf_ben-xvi_spe_20060311_spiritual-exercises.html.

11 Pope Francis, *Evangelii Gaudium (The Joy of the Gospel)*, November 24, 2013, http://w2.vatican.va/content/francesco/en/apost_exhortations/documents/papa-francesco_esortazione-ap_20131124_evangelii-gaudium.html, par. 120.

12 Second Vatican Ecumenical Council, *Decree on Ecumenism*, http://www.vatican.va/archive/hist_councils/ii_vatican_council/documents/vat-ii_decree_19641121_unitatis-redintegratio_en.html, par. 11.

13 Pope Francis, *Evangelii Gaudium*, par 164.

14 Fr. Tom Forrest, C.Ss.R., *Move It Out!: Sharing the Word of Christ with Zeal* (United Kingdom: Word Among Us Press, 2004).

15 Pope Paul VI, *Evangelii Nuntiandi*, par. 41.

16 Ibid., par. 46.

17 Fr. Almire Pichon, quoted in *The Letters of St. Therese of Lisieux*, vol. 2 (Washington, DC: ICS Publications, 1982), 767.

18 Pope John Paul II, *Catechesi Tradendae (On Catechesis in Our Time)*, 1979, http://w2.vatican.va/content/john-paul-ii/en/apost_exhortations/documents/hf_jp-ii_exh_16101979_catechesi-tradendae.html, par. 25.

19 Pope Francis, *Evangelii Gaudium*, par. 13.

20 Rick Warren, "Help Your Members Prepare a Testimony," Pastors .com, September 27, 2017, http://pastors.com/help-your-members-prepare-a-testimony/ (accessed December 6, 2017).

21 Pope Paul VI, *Evangelii Nuntiandi*, par. 14.

22 Ibid, par. 75.

23 Pope John Paul II, *Redemptoris Missio*, par. 21.

24 Pope Francis, *The Joy of the Gospel*, par. 259.

25 CCC 1302–1303.

26 For further discussion on how a sacrament can be valid and yet its power "unreleased," read Fr. Raniero Cantalamessa, "The Baptism in the Spirit, A Grace for the Whole Church," https://zenit.org/articles/father-cantalamessa-explains-why-baptism-in-the-spirit-is-a-gift-for-the-whole-church/ (accessed December 6, 2017).

27 Saint Louis Marie de Montfort, *True Devotion to the Blessed Virgin* (Montfort Publications, 1984), 127.

28 Pope John XXIII, *Humanae salutis*, December 25, 1961, text available in Latin at https://w2.vatican.va/content/john-xxiii/la/apost_constitutions/1961/documents/hf_j-xxiii_apc_19611225_humanae-salutis.html.

29 Pope Benedict XVI, Message for World Youth Day in Madrid, 2008.

30 Pope Francis, *Evangelii Gaudium*, par. 164.

31 Pope Paul VI, *Evangelii Nuntiandi*, par. 2.

32 Ibid., par. 62.

33 Gregory A. Smith and Alan Cooperman, "The factors driving the growth of religious 'nones' in the U.S.," Pew Research FactTank, September 14, 2016, http://www.pewresearch.org/facttank/2016/09/14/the-factors-driving-the-growth-of-religiousnones-in-the-u-s/ (accessed December 6, 2017).

34 Saint Josemaría Escrivá, *Christ Is Passing By* (1973), 95, http://www.escrivaworks.org/book/christ_is_passing_by.htm (accessed December 6, 2017).

35 Archbishop Adam Exner, homily given at VCCRS Conference, September 29, 1996, http://seminarofhope.org/manual-contents---jan2014.pdf (accessed December 6, 2017).

36 Visit ChristLife.org to view a map of parishes running the Discovering Christ course.

37 Pope Paul VI, *Evangelii Nuntiandi*, par. 14.

38 Pope Francis, *Evangelii Gaudium*, par. 3.

39 John Paul II, *Redemptoris Missio*, par. 46.

About ChristLife

ChristLife equips Catholics for the essential work of evangelization so others might personally encounter Jesus Christ and be transformed into His missionary disciples in the Catholic Church. The ministry partners with dioceses, parishes, and small group leaders who are seeking to answer the Church's call for the New Evangelization through a proven process of parish evangelization and outreach. They developed the ChristLife Series to help all people discover, follow, and share Jesus Christ as members of the Catholic Church.

ChristLife's story began with Dave Nodar, a Catholic layman who during the 1990s regularly presented schools of evangelization in Poland and Slovakia for young adult Catholics from the former Soviet Bloc. Inspired by the call of Pope John Paul II to a new evangelization, Dave approached Cardinal William Keeler, Archbishop of Baltimore, about beginning an evangelization ministry. The Cardinal was enthused, and he recognized ChristLife as an apostolate of the Archdiocese in 1995.

CHRISTLIFE™

CATHOLIC MINISTRY FOR EVANGELIZATION

Contact Us

(888) 498-8474
info@christlife.org
www.christlife.org

Find Us on Social Media

 Facebook ("ChristLifeOrg")

 Twitter ("ChristLifeInc")

 YouTube ("ChristLifeMinistry")

THE CHRISTLIFE SERIES

Discovering Christ

Discovering Christ is a seven-week experience that creates an open door in the parish for people who are searching for the meaning of their lives where they can share the Good News and the personal love of Jesus Christ. To learn more, visit: **www.christlife.org/discover**.

Following Christ

Following Christ is a seven-week journey that builds upon Discovering Christ and provides the tools to help Catholics grow in discipleship, including daily personal prayer, hearing God in Scripture, the power of the sacraments, forgiving one another, spiritual warfare, etc. To learn more, visit: **www.christlife.org/follow**.

Sharing Christ

Sharing Christ is a seven-week mission that equips Catholics with the practical skills to proclaim the Gospel, draw others into a personal relationship with Jesus Christ, and invite them to become His disciples as members of the Church. To learn more, visit: **www.christlife.org/share**.

About the Authors

Dave Nodar is a frequent speaker in dioceses, parishes, and other organizations in the USA and internationally. He is a content developer and speaker for the Discovering Christ, Following Christ, and Sharing Christ series, as well as co-author of *Discover Christ* and *Follow Christ* and author of *Characteristics of the New Evangelization.* His passion is to help others to know the love of God the Father in Jesus Christ through the transforming power of the Holy Spirit. Dave and his wife, Ely, have seven adult children and eight grandchildren and live in Ellicott City, Maryland. Their desire is to bear witness together to the good news of God's love, mercy, and life-changing presence. Dave enjoys hiking with Ely and wishfully dreaming of opportunities to go fishing!

Dianne Davis began her career in banking, advancing to Vice President of both Bank of New York and M&T Bank. She married her husband, John, whom she met in high school, and they have two sons. Even though it looked like she had all she was striving for, inside she felt a longing for something more. In March 2002, two women came to her office looking for a business loan and ended up sharing the Gospel with her. Later that night, Dianne committed her life to Jesus. She eventually left her career in banking and is now a Catholic evangelist leading friends and strangers to Christ. She serves as ChristLife's NY Regional Director, conference speaker, and teacher on the Sharing Christ series.

Fr. Erik Arnold is pastor of Our Lady of Perpetual Help in Ellicott City, Maryland, and ChristLife's liaison to Archbishop William Lori of Baltimore. He earned a Licentiate in Sacred Theology from the Pontifical Gregorian University and was ordained a priest for the Archdiocese of Baltimore in 1999. He is a speaker for the Discovering Christ, Following Christ, and Sharing Christ series. As a pastor, he has run the ChristLife series in his parish multiple times and seen great fruit come from it as people's lives are changed by the Lord Jesus and the power of the Gospel. Fr. Erik loves to escape to the outdoors to get recharged, especially through hiking and kayaking, as well as drawing support from family, priest friends, and a good meal.